LIFE IS NEW ALL THE TIME

HOW TO SEIZE LIFE'S OPPORTUNITIES BY NAVIGATING CHANGE

GERMAN E. VELASCO

Order this book online at www.trafford.com
or email orders@trafford.com

Most Trafford titles are also available at major online book retailers.

Print information available on the last page.

ISBN: 978-1-4907-8872-2 (sc)
ISBN: 978-1-4907-8873-9 (e)

Trafford rev. 05/04/2018

www.trafford.com

North America & international
toll-free: 1 888 232 4444 (USA & Canada)
fax: 812 355 4082

CONTENTS

To my Father, the man who knew that love
was the best reason to live a life.

FOREWORD

I know my children have difficulty answering the question, *What does your father do for a living?*, if they perceive that the question is meant to elicit a summary view of me. My children cannot describe their father by pointing to his occupation. And, this difficulty at describing me by what I do, I admit, has been very deliberate on my side and makes me proud of my richly lived life.

Currently, I coach people dealing with change in their lives: I offer life coaching, career coaching and divorce coaching. But, I am also working hard to get my movie-making passion to become more tangible. And, just as my children have experienced the good life of being the children of the Governor of La Paz when I held that role many years ago, they have also experienced the not-so-good life of being the children of a clumsy man who lost entire businesses more than once. My children have also experienced a father who has reinvented himself from the glamorous title of Presidential Advisor, to being a more modest professional in a different land—an interpreter and mediator.

Long ago, their father was an architect and builder, and then, after obtaining a master's degree, he took on urban planning before gravitating toward public policy. He became a consultant for exciting-sounding organizations like the World Bank and the United Nations. Then, when something sparked his fascination for political strategy, he did that too. Perhaps a common thread of public service was present in their father's life for a certain number of years: I was a presidential advisor to three different presidents, Secretary of Housing, Governor, planning consultant, and political consultant.

But other passions have also been in play, like writing, or my often changing new small businesses, with one business being replaced a year or two later by a new creation. Small businesses have ranged from a translation company in Washington, D.C. (with several federal agencies as clients) to offering cross-cultural training for lawyers and judges in Colorado and Nevada. From designing and marketing handcrafts, to publishing a magazine and turning a profit from the first issue, to buying a big house and renovating it into a profitable small shopping center with sixteen different stores, to losing the entire business in the next no-so-brilliant move. From directing documentaries to owning a small production house. This reinventing was an absolute necessity as their father resisted the status of a nine-to-five employee. Sometimes, of course, this resistance came at absurd risks and costs. There was always a high degree of change for my children, with their father living and working in different cities and countries.

Maybe this book will explain what many people would perceive as my apparently erratic behavior. Yet, for me, it was never erratic. Yes, it has been and it remains a life of exploration, adventure, diversity and relative risk. It adheres to a view that we should never compromise when we feel that something is not really meant for us.

I feel that my responsibility as a father and my love for my children were the only boundaries to not taking even larger risks and not exploring other dimensions of life. Nevertheless, adventure and change were always a natural environment for my children, and I was very intentional about it. Every new trip was adventurous: We crossed ferocious rivers, traveled to places where there were no roads, and spent months looking for an alleged treasure.

We had fun while living life.

At some points in my life I have even lost sight of the intrinsic value of my current accomplishments. I have folded several businesses just to move to a new place and start a new business, without the necessary patience to sell the old one. Sitting behind the same desk was never my goal, but out of these losses, big lessons were learned along the way. Sometimes, the lessons were painful; most of the time, I continued forward with an unbreakable optimism and no regrets.

I know this lifestyle is not a recipe for what the world sees as stability, but it is a proven recipe for a full life, an opportunity to taste life in all of its beauty and harshness. If we must laugh, cry and suffer big blows in life anyway, we may as well do so following the paths that we ourselves find interesting. We owe it to ourselves.

Change has been my constant, and understanding its power has helped me become a good support to my friends and clients who are in the midst of trying to move on.

Ultimately, I am not speaking here of change for the sake of variety, or of change as entertainment. I am speaking of change from the viewpoint of reclaiming something within that may have become deeply buried by an inaccurate self-definition, or by a misplaced sense of responsibility, or by past experiences of trauma.

Transformative change is, in the end, an expression of the freedom to be happy. Not happy in the next life or at some undefined point in the future, but freedom to be happy here and now. How we see ourselves, and how we see life and the world, determines whether or not we allow ourselves to change and therefore experience joy.

I will have much more to say about change in the pages to come, but before continuing any further, I would be remiss if I did not express my thanks to the people who have helped me with this book. I thank Ellen Alderton from Apple Pie Writing, my editor. I also wish to express my deep gratitude to my friends Kathy Janak and Vivi Pena y Lillo for support and inspiration, and to Chossi Balanza for her support, inspiration and patience. Very special thanks to my four inspiring children, Maira, German, Diego and Pablo, who never cease to surprise me with their ability to navigate change and conquer their dreams so naturally.

German Velasco
Boulder, Colorado

INTRODUCTION: ARE YOU AGILE AT CHANGE?

Too often, too many people spend long periods of their lives with a burning feeling that they are perfectly capable of doing better if they could only change something important. They also live with the deep intuition that they are capable of doing what it would take. Yet they stay still.

Agility at change and the ability to adapt to change, versus a tendency to stagnate or to resist change, are two opposite approaches to living life. One approach creates a rich, fulfilling life, while the other creates a life filled with struggles and frustrations. One approach is big and wide; the other, small and narrow.

Others live happily making their dreams come true, oblivious to the fact that their biggest skill is being agile at change. If life were a song, those who are naturally agile at change are those who seem to be in tune, while the ones who react poorly to change get stuck all the time and seem to be offbeat.

Learning to be agile at change is possible and it can transform lives beyond imagination. Gaining awareness of how we resist change—and why—is an important requirement in order to acquire this skill. This book discusses the reasons why change is so fundamental. Also, you will find in this book the tools, the maps, and the practical steps for making change a way of life—the happier life you were meant to lead.

CHANGE AND YOU

Change in this universe is inescapable: for you and for me and for every living and non-living thing in it. Change is taking place constantly. We change whether we want to or not. But also, everything around us changes whether we want or not.

Understanding certain keys to how life works can make immense differences in the quality of life we live. One of these important keys is grasping the fact that people must change in tune with our surrounding or else we will collide. If we are rigid to the winds of change, we are guaranteeing that somewhere, sometime there will be friction or collision in our lives.

This book's main hypothesis is that most of us do not live even close to our fullest potential because we fail to understand the transcendental impact of constant change in life. Another hypothesis of this book is that most of us walk through life unaware of the anchors that keep us from making small and large fundamental changes in our lives, therefore preventing us from realizing our dreams.

These anchors are many and they come in all shapes and sizes. An anchor can be the fear that you will not be able to get another job like the one you have, even though you hate every aspect of your job. Dreaming and knowing that you could start your own business but not fully trusting your instincts suggests another anchor; in this case, the lack of trust in your instincts. Another anchor can be a feeling that you are not really worth something better, and therefore you are staying in a tortuous relationship with a partner or a boss. Another example of an anchor would be the belief that you must endure and persist no matter what; therefore, you stay in an abusive marriage watching how your children are also living a miserable life. In all of these cases, endurance is not a virtue anymore. It is a blinder that keeps you in a stupid situation for the wrong reasons while sacrificing precious time.

This book aims to make you aware of your anchors and help you find their sources so you can become a freer person who is agile at change and able to flow with life in a positive rhythm.

Living a life agile at change is directly conducive to having the ability to get your goals accomplished, regardless of scale, versus living a life according to the crippling approach where you get stuck over and over again, waste precious time and opportunities in a cyclical fashion, and becoming trapped in the groove of a small life.

THE TRAP OF THE FAMILIAR

Sometimes the anchor that keeps you in a situation that is far from ideal is a preference for the comfort of the familiar over the discomfort of exploring new grounds. Again, examples might be a job you do not like, a city you do not like or a toxic relationship.

Also, clinging to the familiar can be expressed in attachment to the initial dynamics of a personal relationship, then, failing to evolve when the relationship itself evolves into something different. This latter example makes me think of a song where you start in perfect harmony and once it changes tempo, you fall off beat and begin to sound off. Life offers so much more when we are willing to venture to the unfamiliar for a short period of time—until the new context becomes familiar, of course.

STAGNATION HARDENS

The longer people stagnate when facing an important need to change, the harder it gets to eventually move forward. Stagnation tends to have an effect on people like cement drying. Those, who naturally or consciously understand the power of change as a constant, on the other hand, feed on their victories and failures and they keep making bigger and bigger leaps. They quickly distance themselves from those who live stagnant lives.

The more a person becomes afraid of venturing into the unknown, the more he or she will feel afraid to fail, ignoring that failing is an essential part of learning to fly.

NINJAS OF CHANGE

A ninja of change in this book is a flexible person, quick to adapt to life's inevitable changes; one who also deeply understands the intrinsic value of change and one who pilots his or her own changes masterfully. The ninjas of change and adaptation to whatever is necessary leave the rest of us with comparatively miniature lives. People of change enjoy far more life experiences than those who live in the groove of getting stuck every time life demands from them an urgent change, let alone an adventurous change.

Agility at change happens to be a trait of most people who are outliers, accomplishers, and go-getters. But, most importantly, agility at change can make for happier people.

One excellent example these days is Elon Musk. Musk has lived several lifetimes in his forty-six years of age. He has been involved in PayPal, Tesla Motors, Space X, Solar City, Hyperloop, The Boring Company, Neuralink, Open AI and The Musk Foundation. This is only his public life.

But even with less famous people, if you look around your world you will start finding dramatic differences between, for example, Liz, who is thirty years old and has visited twenty-five countries, has lived in three different ones, has biked a full European country and has walked the entire Pacific Coast of the United States in four months—while she lives an otherwise normal life working as a pharmacist. Yet, in the same building, you find your other friend who is fifty-seven years old and a brilliant accountant who has changed jobs twice in his career, has never traveled abroad, and who complains every day about how much he dislikes his job. He is brilliant at his profession, and he could get a better job any day, but inexplicably he does not move out of the miserable little hole in life where he is stuck.

I agree with Eleanor Roosevelt's advice: "Do something that scares you every day." We just need to tear down our blinders to come to see and understand the difference between approaching life as a creature of change or as a seeker of permanence. In a universe where change is the only constant, one of these approaches is like trying to stop the rain by banging your head against a wall.

A SIMPLE METHOD

Throughout this book, I provide you with a method to become agile at change and to get goals accomplished. At times, the method presented in this book may seem extremely simple; that is because it truly is simple. It is a recipe with very few ingredients, but each ingredient must be taken seriously. Hopefully, you will also find yourself surprised by the magic of this simplicity and the results it yields.

This book is also about those factors that tend to detour us from the path of success, and about developing the necessary discipline to attain big changes in life. These factors are not only those anchors that we have briefly described already, but also factors like sheer distraction or inability to properly prioritize the use of our daily time. This book provides insight and helps you get to know yourself better. It helps you find your own tools for not getting distracted or lost in your quest, whether your quest is to spend more time with your family or to take a trip around the world or to change careers. It helps you to identify those tools that may work best for you and not necessarily for someone else. It empowers you with a very tangible and down-to-earth strategy.

> "Change is not merely necessary to life - it is life."
> Alvin Toffler

NO NEED TO BE A HERO

This book's approach to achieving powerful changes in your life does not require that you first turn into a superhero or a gambler. Many people have the discipline that took me decades to develop to keep from jumping too soon into a new and exciting project before finishing the last very exciting project; or to learn the art of putting things on the back burner and methodologically come back and working on two or three projects alternatively. It is absolutely possible to make changes without burning your bridges. Although, sometimes, a big jump may call for you to burn a bridge to a past context. Either way, making big changes in your own life is empowering and exciting.

Yes, courage is also an important ingredient for piloting change in your own life, but this book's method offers a lot more than simply improving your self-esteem and encouraging you to jump off a cliff. I will try to give you tools that help you with the actual task. And, also, exploring the factors that may be holding you back may require the courage to look at your past, to understand it and acknowledge new discoveries.

The reward is the unleashing of fantastic potential that can bring you to a completely different level of existence. So, arguably, jettisoning anchors that may be holding you back is a critical step to accomplishing important changes in life.

BACK TO REDISCOVERING OUR HUMAN POTENTIAL

I find it extremely interesting how human history tends to reoccur in cycles that resemble one another. We seem to be at the dawn of a new era where we need to once again tap into our full human potential. Wake up calls of all sorts seem to be ringing as reminders of the many fundamental values we have abandoned, I suspect, since the start of the Industrial Revolution. We must remind ourselves that each and every human being is unique and very different from the amazing machines that have been the objects of our love for over a century. We have been programming ourselves for a mindset that constrains our creative and free human nature to narrow utilitarian paths.

Artificial Intelligence is pushing us to differentiate ourselves from machines—precisely by tapping into our multidimensional capacities, our non-linear thinking, our creativity, and our abilities to evolve, change and grow in dormant or semi-forgotten areas such intuition and spirit.

In the 14th, 15th and 16th Centuries, Renaissance humanism spread across Western Europe as a reaction to a period dominated by Utilitarianism. Now, in the 21st Century, we seem to be feeling the pressures of a long era of side effects of industrialization and mass production. We are experiencing an unexpected leap into technologies that are beyond our complete comprehension and ability to manage ideally. This leap into new technologies is leading us toward a very unpredictable future.

The 15th Century Renaissance produced a person who is considered one of the most diversely talented individuals ever to have lived, Leonardo Da Vinci. This man knew that life is excitingly broad and full of questions that are waiting for answers around every corner. In the sixty-seven years that he lived, this human being—who obviously did not see himself as his profession or occupation—produced gifts for humanity in the forms of invention, painting, cartography, architecture, sculpting, science, music, mathematics, engineering, literature, anatomy, geology, astronomy, botany, writing and history.

We should remember Da Vinci more often when we question whether it would be too weird to go from being a lawyer to becoming a painter or from being a mechanic to becoming a nurse. He did it all. You are equipped to do that too, once you are free from whatever restrains you or delays you in tackling change when you need it or you want it.

"Men go abroad to wonder at the heights of mountains, at the huge waves of the sea, at the long courses of the rivers, at the vast compass of the ocean, at the circular motions of the stars, and they pass by themselves without wondering." Saint Augustine.

RIDING THE WIND OR FIGHTING THE WIND

The entire success or failure for landing an aircraft depends on maneuvering at the correct angle in regard to this invisible thing called air. In fact, people who resist change and remain stubborn are making a choice similar to crashing versus successfully landing a plane.

We need to practice change constantly in every possible area of our lives. One of the most basic and practical applications of riding rather than fighting with life is to gracefully accept those things that come to us and that we cannot change.

Look around you at the people you know and notice how, if life were a horse, some approach life by violently and roughly handling the animal while others pet it, befriend it, and ride it gracefully. Then observe who seems to live a happier life.

You will also notice that those who lash out violently all the time at life (and get hit back by life) are the people who are very prompt at defining themselves as "I am the type of person who…" or "I am really bad at…" or "I am horrible at business because I'm an artist." People who see themselves as having been born in a set way will struggle with life. Such people immediately see the impossibility of things: "Yes, but they are probably closed on Saturdays." "Yes but it is probably hard to get …" "I bet it is not easy…"

Many people ride on an imaginary linear track with taste only for one type of music, one color, one drink, one culture. The longer these people remain living that false story, the more rigid they become, distancing themselves from their potential to grow wings and fly in life.

RELAXING INTO ACCEPTANCE

On a snowy winter day, we can find the beauty in the white and the cold or we can choose to complain and kick the wall for hours without any response from the weather. This applies to an immense number of circumstances in life. Once you develop this approach of acceptance of what is beyond your reach, you will be surprised by how pleasant life can be. You will see how many more good days versus bad days you have.

But life also brings us many inevitably sad passages such as the death of a loved one. Of course it is terribly hard to find the beauty in something like this. (Unlike how we were able to with a snowy day.)

However bad the occurrence, we still have our choice of response to what happens. For example, we can choose to focus on feeling the love that lasts forever in our hearts, rather than labeling the loss only as a tragedy. We can appreciate that having shared life with a great human being can only be a gain.

When my father passed away three years ago, I realized there was no way I would not miss him for the rest of my life. I accepted that. Then, I realized that his love for us, his family, had been so gigantic that having had this human being as a father would be a plus throughout my life. With this realization, there was only room for gratitude. The intensity of my love for my father and his love for me have not diminished a drop over the years. When I miss him too much, I talk with him and sometimes—half sad and half happy, feeling this love—I let some tears out. I may be driving some picturesque country road at the moment. There is nothing else I can do but to live these feelings when they revisit me.

SHIFT TO POSITIVE

Shifting your focus toward the positive things that life still offers you after a big loss is not a form of denial. It is a legitimate and objective tool to pull yourself out of the hell of regret and guilt over something that you can do absolutely nothing about.

After losing my largest business accomplishment—the one that had made me feel so secure for the future and very smart—I picked Washington, D.C. to land and reinvent myself. In D.C., I had no friends, relatives or contacts. It was winter. I was feeling depressed for the first time in my life. Everything seemed to have crumbled to pieces rapidly. I was penniless, alone in this city, missing my family and friends, not sure any more about the validity of my decisions, including having picked this city. The road before me to a "normal life" looked like a climb of an Everest-size mountain.

During this time period, I experienced an important revelation. While standing in line at a bank to apply for a two-thousand-dollar loan, a man about my age walked into the bank with the help of another person. Walking seemed excruciating for him. He was very well dressed, he looked wealthy, and he also looked very ill. A weighty and pertinent thought assaulted me from every angle as fast as Jackie Chang cornering a bad guy: I did not have the right to feel miserable. I had literally lost every financial asset in my life, but I had my health, my children, my parents, my family and my friends, and all I needed was to start over again!

SHIFT TO GRATEFUL

Yes, it was a drag to be financially back at square one with four growing children, but I had twice the force, the need and the experience that I had had ten years before. After that morning in that bank, I have never allowed myself the luxury of self-pity again. There was only room for gratefulness. As it always happens, someone was willing to believe in my idea. In Washington I met Jeff Kline, a bright entrepreneur, and certainly a man of flexible mind who provided radio services to the federal government. We added translations to his services and I subcontracted my work from my rapidly created brand new company.

Six months later I brought the rest of the family to D.C. Less than a year later, I discovered that my entire business could be run via phone and internet. We moved to St. Augustine, Florida—a block from the beach with half the cost of living of D.C.

THE EARLY LOCKS WE PLACE ON OUR FREEDOM

Childhood is inevitably hard for most people. It is a time of total dependence on others. We as children are completely vulnerable and truly at the mercy of a good parent or adult.

In modern societies this vulnerability is even greater, as we do not have a tribe around us. A tribe is a much safer environment for a child. If parents fail, there are grandparents, uncles, aunts, neighbors, etcetera. The safety net that protects childhood is far larger in more collective societies, and the results are absolutely undeniable. In our modern, more individualistic societies, most children are truly living a risky gamble; they either have good parents or childhood can be hell. And even with the best possible parents, parents are normally too busy, too confused, too unprepared and doing their very best at something that comes without a manual, in a world that is far from forgiving.

So, without exceptions, with bigger or smaller doses of luck, there is plenty of trauma from childhood for all of us. Unfortunately, most of us also ignore or deny these traumas and fail to tackle them face-on as soon as possible.

Old trauma sits there defining us in ways that may be exactly the opposite of what we need in order to be flexible and agile at change. We set tight locks to certain doors that could come in very handy in adult life, and we make our path narrow, rigid and limited in options due to reasons that truly are nonexistent. Our life becomes a reaction to something that is not even there anymore. That's what trauma is. The menace is long gone, but the fear is present and very real.

SHAPING OUR PERSONALITY

Often, we make these early unconscious choices of locking doors with a similarly unconscious pledge to never try X again or to never trust Y again. For example, a person who felt abandoned as a child will try to never experience that same feeling of abandonment again—even if in adult life the possibilities for feeling like an abandoned child are not prevalent any longer. The effort to avoid re-living the feeling will likely dictate decisions in adult life that may not always be the most suitable for that person's adult goals.

These "never again" locks become so solid that they shape our personality, define our boundaries, and tell us to stay on familiar ground only. Those phantoms make us prisoners in tiny linear lives. Living becomes a narrow scary path where we need to touch the walls on both sides all the time. Flying is out of the question.

Imagine now how wingless most of us begin our journey. Unfortunately, it does not get better, as these traits cement themselves in many ways. We walk life oblivious to its true beauty and possibilities.

So, tackling our childhood traumas early in life is one of the smartest decisions young adults can make. Knock on the door of a good therapist without any sense of embarrassment (or with embarrassment if you prefer), and go and do it. We all need to do this; only smart and courageous people deal with their childhood traumas, and they are many, many steps closer to having the ability to understand and become change-ninjas and discover how beautiful life really is.

LIVING INSIDE THE WRONG COAT

Millions and millions of people live uncomfortably every day, doing what they do, similarly to constantly wearing a coat two sizes too small.

By not taking some risks and experimenting in life, we could end up stuck in the wrong life. On the other hand, walking the extra mile to find the life that fits us best eventually translates into the ability to feel joyful about what we do every day.

> "Your work is going to fill a large part of your life, and the only way to be truly satisfied is to do what you believe is great work. And the only way to do great work is to love what you do. If you have not found it yet, keep looking. Do not settle. As with all matters of the heart, you'll know when you find it." Steve Jobs

Living inside the wrong coat causes a great deal of unhappiness and goes against our human nature.

As a young boy, I hated the notion that someone had decided on my behalf that I needed to attend school for twelve years. In my youthful way of thinking, it was a violation of my freedom. Not having a choice made me constantly feel like a prisoner. Dropping out of school in my family would have been the equivalent of sawing off a leg in front of my parents. So, that option was not on the table. Nevertheless, to my good fortune, after fifth grade I discovered the escape valve for my uncomfortable life: change. Over the next seven years, I changed schools five times.

The novelty of meeting new people, new teachers and new kinds of schools turned out to be a blessing that carried me through the otherwise intolerable twelve-year journey. The blessing came in the

13

form of the numbers of people and the social diversity I ended up encountering during those years. I have many, many school reunions and literally hundreds of life-long friends just from that era. One time while still in high school, a gang assaulted two of us in a street in La Paz. It was dark and we were in the wrong neighborhood. Surrounded by about twenty youth who were ready to pummel us, a voice from the back said, "Let them go!" A former classmate from one of my many schools approached, said "Hello," and we walked away.

After high school, I was truly free of wearing the wrong coat. Everything became possible in my mind after high school was over, especially when I found myself at eighteen years of age, working odd jobs in Geneva, Madrid, and Rome, and supporting myself. Life felt large and beautiful and it has never stopped feeling that way.

The next time I felt like I was wearing the wrong coat again was after architecture school. I had made a bad choice; I felt it clearly in my heart. I did not feel like the wisest individual, because I had decided to follow through with that career based on a notion that after so much work and sweat and money, I had to carry on—no matter how.

After that frustrating experience of not fitting well with my chosen profession, I have tried not to wear the wrong coat again. And, as I've explained, it has not been always easy. Nevertheless, I have done my best to remain faithful to my unfolding discoveries of what life has to offer at any given place and time.

When you detect signs of discomfort with your life (the wrong coat), it is important to take the time aside to find the source of the discomfort. Sometimes we are too busy feeding our family and paying bills or pursuing a career while holding a job, and we do not allow ourselves that necessary moment to stop and see what part of our life is asking for a change.

ROCKS ON THE TRACKS, LANDSLIDES AND PLAN B

People who resist change tend to live life on a track. This approach is similar to the difference between traveling on a train versus enjoying the change-ninja advantages of an all-terrain vehicle. The person who is rigid of mind will see an obstacle and, because he is traveling on a fixed track, will have to stop the trip. The flexible change-ninja will see an obstacle, quickly assess alternatives, choose one and keep traveling.

It takes constant practice to train your reflexes in your body. The same is true of the reflexes in your brain. I recommend trying fun daily practices that make you more and more malleable to the big changes. In your mind, quickly open the door to plan B or plan C before frustration or panic strikes—for any situation, big or small.

For some people, thinking of a plan B and C comes as second nature—a reflex. For others, it is second nature to give up immediately after plan A fails, even in small day-to-day things. It happens all the time. Something does not go the way we expected, and frustration is the first response.

When we give in and let frustration or panic take over, we often cancel very good plans or get rid of excellent ideas just because one variable has failed along a path. But it can be even worse. Sometimes not giving up on the possibility of an alternative solution can make a life or death difference.

German E. Velasco

A PLAN B FROM HEAVEN

On one occasion I was asked by the President to mediate a conflict between the Ministry of Agriculture and a coca growers' union, the second largest in the country. In a mountainous region in the sub-tropics, the protesters had been blocking a main access road from the mountains to the plains of the Amazon basin. There were three-thousand people camping in makeshift tents along two miles of treacherous road, known as the Death Road due to its narrow curves and high cliffs.

There were twelve people in our government commission. The negotiations began around four in the afternoon, and by seven at night, the leader of the protestors was losing control of the crowd. The government's proposed solution had proven to be more of an insult than a plausible course of action.

It was well after dark and, in the small makeshift stage lit by one lightbulb connected to a car battery, people took turns suggesting how to kill the twelve of us. A couple of journalists, cameramen and the nearby town priest completed the group of those terrified.

The situation was especially dire because the strikers had been waiting for attention from the government for seven long days, there was plenty of alcohol in their bloodstreams, and there were many guns in their tents. The air was filled with sounds of speakers venting against the government and some hinting at the failure of their local leader. I whispered to the government group not to take the microphone anymore because one wrong word could ignite the already fragile situation. I also gave orders to disguise Oswaldo Antezana, the main leader in the anti-drug camp; luckily, he had not spoken in the afternoon. Now, if discovered, he was the perfect first victim to be thrown off the cliffs by the angry mob.

Suddenly, one of the many enraged speakers uttered something that sounded to me like a plan B from heaven. He said, "We should keep these people hostage until we consult with our national leader."

In a flash of desperate inspiration, I moved three steps to the leader of the protests, who was clearly frightened. I said to him, "Take the microphone and clearly accept that proposal to keep us hostages. Order that we sleep in Yolosa, the town down the road. Be very authoritative!"

Miraculously, he did exactly that. The furious crowd was caught by surprise by a temporary resolution. There was silence and, as I was holding my breath in suspense, someone pulled me -it was Gaston, friend and member of my crew. He made me walk in the dark to meet the rest of the now hostage group. They put us, standing, in the back of a pick-up truck and slowly started rolling down the road amid insults and occasional whacking with long sticks. Anything felt a lot a lot better than being dead.

Over the next five days we negotiated a deal, about seven miles away from the heat of the crowd, which felt like a beach vacation compared to facing a menu of options for how to be executed.

Resourceful people are creative people, and creative people are natural change-ninjas. The exercise here is to practice your resourcefulness muscle by blocking anxiety and panic and immediately jumping to potential solutions in your mind.

Practice with small things like a cancelled appointment: Option one, complain, curse and get deeply annoyed (a recipe for a ruined afternoon). Option two, feel like you have gained a slice of free time to enjoy doing something you never have time to do, like reading, walking, or exploring a neighborhood, a museum, or a store stocked with a kind of goods you never thought you would like.

These are small ways to ride the winds of life. Once your brain knows that such possibilities exist, you will become a natural, because opening alternative doors will become a reflexive reaction.

Just like looking before crossing the street, you will find yourself smiling and developing plan B and plan C in everything that is not resulting according to plan A. This kind of thinking will keep you in control of the wheel of your life, with the added benefit of discovering that quite often plans B or C or F turn out to be a gift from heaven, making plan A look like a poor option after all.

CLINGING TO MISERY

In my coaching work, it is not unusual to find clients who are parked in situations of misery as if by God's command. We are not always conscious of the anchors that prevent us from making important changes in our lives, and they hold us frozen in place. The reasons for these anchors can be very diverse as we said before, depending on our upbringing and past experiences. Yet, in general, it is basic human nature to cling to security as well to remain in familiar territory— even when that territory has little if anything to offer.

Even if that comfort zone is not truly comfortable, as long as it is familiar, it will try to play a trick on us and keep us stuck. People like familiarity; the unfamiliar is stressful. That's why the large majority of the human race is not Christopher Columbus or Elon Musk.

Psychotherapist Katherine Schafler writes, "If you're used to feeling that people disappoint you, that you're unhealthy, that you're unattractive, that you're not smart or that you're always broke, then you know how to feel those things. You know exactly what the feeling is like, and though it may not be a desirable feeling, it is highly predictable. Letting go of what's familiar to you is like transplanting yourself into a new land where you do not speak the language."

Something in her childhood had convinced one of my clients, Claudia (not her real name), that she should always be in the supporting role. She mistakenly believed she should never be the star of her own life. Later, she worked hard to come to terms with the realization that she had given up her biggest dreams and her extraordinary artistic talent for twenty-five years for her husband's sake—a man who felt professionally threatened. Her husband kept tight psychological control on her by manipulating her feelings of low self-worth. In spite of that pressure, Claudia was the family's money maker, the caretaker of two children, and she was brilliant at most things she tackled. But her most beloved dreams were put on hold for a quarter century while she supported her husband's career. In turn, her husband's career never produced great results, but managed to kill Claudia's potential career.

Understanding the reasons why someone with all the tools in the world sometimes willingly surrenders to someone who would live off another person's blood is puzzling. Digging into Claudia's past, the patterns created by a submissive mother shone like spotlights in the night.

Whether these anchors are big or small, deep or on the surface, it is important (and very exciting) to find them.

> "The mass of men lead lives of quiet desperation.
> What is called resignation is confirmed desperation."
> Henry David Thoreau

LIFE IS NEW ALL THE TIME

Only by embodying change we can live life in the moment. Only by grasping the ever-changing nature of life can we experience every instant as something legitimately different from the past.

Most of us live in a box observing reality as something we already know, when, truly, we cannot know reality. We tend to live each new moment as if the new moment was already known and familiar.

This is an illusion; the new moment is brand new. We can only know reality the moment it unfolds in front of us with us in it. And that is precisely the necessary understanding that allows us to plug ourselves into reality as something new and free from the past.

When we truly acknowledge the constantly changing nature of life, we also understand the miraculous opportunity that is presented to us at every instant.

YOUR NEW YEAR BEGINS EVERY DAY

I have not been discussing abstract philosophies; what I am describing is tangible. When a person truly embodies change, he is totally free from his past. He is able to choose again, and he is able to choose to follow the same course or do something completely different. Feeling no ties, life is truly new all the time. This encounter with our true freedom is indeed profound and life changing.

You are free to act exactly according to how you feel and what you want at any given moment. You do not need to act according to what you may have thought in the past was the right way or the only way. You are the commander of your life: not your past, not your stories, not your beliefs. You.

Nothing is as fascinating as life itself. No fiction competes with this journey where we are offered so much in so many dimensions. But we have to be willing to come out of the bubble of "I already know that" in order to avoid a life that simply repeats our first experiences over and over again.

We can avoid the repetition of something we have lived before by choosing to face reality in the moment. We must be aware of the fact that we tend to create concepts about things we experience. For example, because we are familiar with one tree, we assume that we are familiar with all trees. (When no tree on earth is identical to the next!) Or, I may have decided that my friend Joe is a boring person, and that preconception of my poor friend Joe blocks me—like a glass wall—from truly experiencing Joe every time we are together.

LIFE AS A KAISEKI DINNER

You may have heard of or tried Kaiseki Ryoir, an exquisite dining experience that is found mostly in Kyoto, Japan.

The entire dinner is a fete for the senses. Atmosphere, timing, sound, color, texture and, of course, taste are all carefully planned and managed. This is a seasonal meal prepared from scratch by a chef while you are eating the previous course. Ingredients are not duplicated across the courses, and different cooking methods are used for each course.

The reason I bring up this dining experience is because it perfectly illustrates the richness that life can offer to any of us when we are fully present in the moment. The Kaiseki's success depends on keeping the guest fully focused and engaged in the experience—in this case, a multicourse meal served over a period of several hours.

We can live our lives with the awareness that each moment is precious, each experience is unique—even if the moment resembles what we lived yesterday. With this understanding, we can grasp how life opens up, brand new and all the time, right in front of us like a gate into the unknown.

MISSED A TRAIN? TAKE THE NEXT ONE

Many years ago my wife told me, "I swear that in my next life I will come back as a singer." It took me a few minutes to react. But to make this story short, after that incident many years ago, she has taken music and voice lessons. Her next present was a guitar. She started playing the guitar and, over the years, she has since become a proficient singer. She enjoys making music as one of her high priority activities. Singing is an intrinsic part of her week and it has been so for close to fifteen years now. She could, instead, have spent the rest of her life thinking that she hadn't been born to sing in this lifetime.

Many people who are natural at change do not even hesitate to resume something that they left unfinished decades ago or to take on something completely new. They just go and do it.

Generally, it is only the image we have of ourselves that puts the brakes on doing something "crazy" like picking up a guitar, taking lessons and starting singing at age forty-five, fifty-four, or sixty-five. Why not?

Think of famous painter Grandma Moses, who started painting approaching her eighties. Or, think of the fabulous singer Andrea Boccelli as a practicing lawyer before he took up his current successful career. Or, think of Joy Behar, show-business sensation, who was teaching high school when she was forty. Even more inspiring, singer Julio Iglesias, who holds at least two Guinness records in albums sold across the world, started his music career in his hospital bed after a car accident truncated his professional soccer career as a goal keeper for Spain's top team… After having completed his studies to become a lawyer. A true change-ninja.

WATCHING OTHERS LIVE EXCITING LIVES

The cost of "becoming" what we do (making our profession our identity) is far more damaging to our ability to live fuller lives than we realize. It is comparable to locking oneself inside a glass cage from which you can observe, admire and wish you could touch what others touch. You come to admire other people's lives while holding the key in your hand and not using it. Outside the cage is the ample and beautiful diversity of experiences that life offers.

I am not saying that everyone devoted to his or her profession is an unhappy person. I am saying that when that profession takes over who you really are, you are missing out on true opportunities to expand your existence. And, who knows? Perhaps you are missing out on chances to even discover your true love in life. How can you know if cherry is your favorite flavor of ice cream if you have never tasted cherry ice cream?

One of my sons gave up close to two hundred thousand dollars in scholarship funds for a Ph.D. in order to make a visionary and courageous career change. With a master's degree in economics in his pocket, he taught himself software development for a year. Then, in a matter of two years, he was making a six-figure salary in his brand new, exciting profession.

STABILITY EQUALS CHANGE

Ironically, if you are a person of change, you will also appreciate and enjoy the stability of those things that we crave and need most (those that we want to last forever, like a good partner, a family or a good community.) The formula for attaining stability in life is not to freeze the moment and cling to it hoping that everything remains as is. The formula to emotional stability is to change in tune with your world.

You must learn to understand your surroundings and adapt your own changing (or evolving) to the change of your loved ones—be they family, spouses, parents, children, your community, your town or your world.

Life is constantly demanding adaptation from us. Much of the suffering in this world is precisely the result of resisting the necessary multidimensional flows of evolution.

Those who flow masterfully with change find this constant reinvention of themselves delightful and fascinating, like a bird who has learned to fly. Life is rich when we allow ourselves to be real beings of change and not attempt to be iron rods.

Because your partner, your family and your community are also changing day by day, if you are in full harmony with their evolution, they will feel like a constant to you, and that is the perfect example of harmony.

Just like a hot air balloon that travels with the wind, it pays to learn to travel with change.

> "Life is like riding a bicycle. To keep your balance, you
> must keep moving." Albert Einstein

Yes, we are all about change and if you are observant, you will learn to recognize the self-destructive impacts of rigid approaches to life. Even something as fabulous as winning the lottery can prove to be fatal for people who cannot handle change. Yes, even that—becoming a millionaire instantly—can be too much change in one gulp for the one who conceives the familiar as stability.

WE SHOULD TRAVEL WITH TIME

From our human vantage point, the way some things appear can deceive us from seeing these things for what they really are. Most of us have experienced a form of mind game where a picture or a magician completely deceives our senses. In the universe around us, often the reality perceived by our senses happens to be dramatically different from what is truly out there. For instance, this huge flat valley that I see from my cabin is not really flat at all. It is curving as part of a sphere resembling a gigantic basketball. Reality is often a slap across the face.

Time is far trickier than the tangible world. Time is a dimension we cannot totally grasp. There are numerous studies about our perception of time. Time seems to pass at a much slower rate for children, while time seems to fly for older adults. Also, time seems to pass at a different rate depending on where we are and what we are doing; yet, it is measured by the same physical instruments.

A thing we can agree upon is that time exists and does not stop. And the biggest mind game here is that somehow we tend to perceive ourselves as a constant, as permanent, while time keeps moving unstoppably.

Now, most studies about how people perceive time show that we capture its passage in blocks or in slices, such as: I am born; I am ten years old; I am fifteen; I am twenty-one; I am thirty-five; I am forty-five; I am fifty; etcetera. Or we clump time into smaller slices, like one year per slice.

But what appears undeniable about time is that it is constant, and it flows in one direction. I believe it is critical to navigate change in life with enough agility that you can learn to travel with time. In this way, you avoid living with the sensation that you are a bystander watching this train called time pass in front of your eyes.

When we understand the passage of time as something not separate from us, our experience of life will change radically. At the age of fifty or sixty a person may say, "Where has the time gone?" or, "How has time done this to me? Yesterday I was young."

The person who has embraced change and managed it will feel like she traveled her entire life riding with time. The person who has not embraced change will find old age to be partly empty and definitely confusing.

Cesar Kuriyama, a master of change who describes himself as a "creative human person," undertook a project where he filmed one second of video every day as part of an ongoing project to collect all the special times in his life. This project is perhaps the most didactic means I have ever seen to grasp the continuous nature of time. (Please watch his Ted Talk.) I strongly recommend playing with this experiment in your own life for at least three months. It heightens self-perception, and is very simple to do: Shoot one second of video per day of your own life, from your point of view.

For our purposes of understanding the transcendental importance of becoming a change-ninja, it is extremely relevant that we dig a little into the fascinating and mysterious dimension of time, which we inhabit. Grasping your own relationship with time will allow you to perceive to what extent you own your present and your future. It will further help you realize that if you do not claim your present and future, they will happen anyway.

TIME IS AN EMPTY CONTAINER

Time is mysterious and precious. It can contain the most treasured moments or it can contain waste. It can contain complete irrelevance or the greatest secrets of life.

And part of the magic of time is that it has no clear rules as to what is the best way to invest it. We do not know if the most treasured moment will be the last conversation with your mother—which seemed relatively irrelevant at the moment—or the day you finished your first book, or the day you sat at the park doing nothing and you met the most wonderful person in your life.

I have no intention here to lecture you on time management, because one of the characteristics of change-ninjas is that they may look like procrastinators when measured by some standards. Or, they may seem inconsistent—as most creative people look to the eyes of the world. Leonardo Da Vinci would leave his work unfinished for months or even years; more than fifteen years in the case of his masterpiece, The Mona Lisa.

I am convinced that understanding time as an empty vessel that you can fill with either gold or garbage is very important. Everything is made inside this vessel. The fabulous laptop at your fingertips, the glorious gold-medal championship, the coffee in your cup, the day you fell in love. All are the result of time constructively invested. And this does not mean that you must be working in your shop all the time. It means: Do not forget time is a fantastic vessel waiting for your wisdom to turn it into your gift to yourself.

UNENDING DISTRACTIONS

In order to get things done today we need to revisit our personal relationship with time and we need to understand a newly spreading phenomena: unending distraction. The problem with this kind of distraction is precisely the unending part of it. Movies, television, watching sports, news, games: They all can and have been distractions for decades, but it has not been until interactive media that the amount of available material to watch has become practically infinite.

I find entertainment without a specific end one of the great threats to people's pursuance of their goals. We cannot take the marvel of YouTube lightly. It is indeed a marvel that has changed the world, but it can also be the poison that fills your precious vessel called time, taking the place of the gold you could offer to the world.

CHANGE HAS NO CONSTANT DIRECTION

Watch out for preconceptions and social programing. Change does not mean going from younger to older and from older to dead. Change in life is a lot more exciting than that! Change is about becoming something different without letting go of your essence. Change is growing into a better human being all the time.

Our evolution is multidimensional, not linear as we often perceive. For example, just consider a single realm, our role in a family: We move from being someone's fragile child to being someone's strong child; we move to being someone's partner and then we move to being someone's parent. We move to seeing our parents leave this life as we greet our children's children in their arrival. In these processes, we are required to take care of those who took care of us when we were fragile.

But notice that in the example above, there is a whole other dimension of growth through change: After going through the growing pains to become adults, eventually, if we want to parent children, in order to be good at the task part of us has to go back to being a child at the same time that we must remain an adult. It is a brand new state of being: the adult/child.

Why do we need to achieve this state of being in order to raise a child? Because raising a child for the rigid person who has forgotten (or has cut ties with his childhood) means he or she is not able to feel like a child anymore. This lends itself to a lot of misunderstanding of the needs of the child. A child connects better with the parent who has a child inside. On the other hand, a parent who never truly evolved from his childhood (yet, is biologically an adult) will lack the necessary vision to guide his child in critical moments.

The same principle applies to growing as a better-suited significant other, or a boss in a company or a leader of a community. It is how we gradually grow after each experience what makes us fit for a new position.

HUMAN-ORGANIZED SYSTEMS DO NOT LIKE CHANGE

We often hear the depressing description of people as creatures of habit. While this description in only partially true, there can be no doubt that part of us pulls us into routines and procedures because they are familiar ways to do something. And, we also live in a society that leans toward standardization and uniformity.

These unhealthy surroundings—that I believe are the result of the Industrial Revolution—not only mislead us into feeling like being a number in society is okay, but they also create a distortion that blocks the immense potential of the average human being.

It is clear to me that any system that is already in place, such as a factory, discourages change, and that is understandable from the standpoint of the guy who is making money out of the factory. But when the "well-oiled machine" philosophy permeates society and turns streets into repeating patterns without any personality, turns housing into suburban cookie-cutter spaces, and turns jobs into repetitive tasks, our nature rebels. Our natural urge for constant creativity and evolution is constrained by a system that works well for those who are not bound by the machinery and are not feeling asphyxiated by routine. (Factory owners tend to have a much more diverse day than their workers.)

So, when you feel that something is not right with your surroundings and it is clashing with a need to experience change and creativity, give yourself credit—you are correct in feeling this internal pressure! Then give your soul an outlet to be creative and constructive, to change and evolve.

What we just said could be explained in a practical and typical modern-day situation: A person is stuck in a horrible non-creative job, stuck by temporary financial necessity (baby twins, a new wife and a recent bankruptcy). In this case, perhaps immediate change of physical environment may not be possible, but changes inside the person may provide an urgently needed internal peace. This person should acknowledge the need for change and prioritize a side activity, such as art, or even start to devote energy towards learning something that could eventually become his new career. Then, there is an open valve and the pressure cooker will have less chances to explode.

NEW EQUALS NEW PROBLEMS?

Yes, yes, yes. There are many areas of life where the equation, "new equals new problems," applies almost religiously. In machinery for instance, it is wise not to introduce too many changes too fast when a machine has proven successful. From cars to airplanes to toaster ovens, the more complex the machine, the more it will tend to evolve slowly. Boeing introduced its Dreamliner, with tons of new technology, about fifty years after its previously most recent successful machine, the 747 Jumbo Jet.

Many people mistakenly carry this approach to their human lives and that causes eventual problems. In human life, some changes are relatively gradual and slow, but other changes may require rearranging something immediately.

Change in this universe occurs at all kinds of rates. We hardly perceive the changes in the mountain outside our window, but it is changing. At the human level, change inside ourselves requires constant observation and reaction. And, always remember, we are not machines.

Most importantly, remind yourself that you are a unique fabulous product in this universe. Not alone, but unique. You and I were created by mechanisms that we can only understand on the surface. No, we cannot fully understand nature, even with all of our centuries of science.

I cannot help but surrender in total humility when I observe and compare our most sophisticated human systems and any nature-created system. Consider the amount of effort necessary to keep human-created systems functioning: from airplanes to Social Security to the U.S. Army to a country. Meanwhile, nature offers us the miracle of a full forest covering dozens of mountains, not ever repeating a tree, a bush, an animal: all populated by unique life, with the entire system connected to its surroundings in an ecosystem, in ways that we have not even begun to comprehend.

We are the products of nature, and therefore it is not a good idea to think of ourselves within merely the parameters we use for our own creations. In doing so, we are placing limits on our true potential. As a product of nature, we cannot get credit for what we are. But, we are surely very powerful beings when we do not constrain ourselves with limited stories or manmade misperceptions.

BE CHANGE

One second on this planet is never the same as the next one, but understanding change is not enough. The theory behind this entire book is that we must embody change as a way of life. We must practice ways that keep us from falling into small grooves before they become deep trenches narrowing our ability to grasp the greatness of life.

Malleability is the key tool to executing those big leaps in life: like changing jobs, like exploring new careers, like improving a relationship with a loved one.

A sign of rigidity is expressed when we have an image of ourselves as someone who was born with unchangeable traits. Some examples of an unchangeable self-image include: "I am not good at math," "I am a clumsy person," and "I am poor."

WE ALL HAVE A CHANCE

Many of the most brilliant mathematical minds, I am sure, where not born or raised to be brilliant in math. Hundreds are the stories of people who struggled with something in childhood, only to excel precisely at that something later in their lives. From dancers to singers, to composers, to scientists. We all have a chance.

I do not oppose the vision that family, culture, era, generation, idiosyncratic experiences and other factors boost some people's success in certain areas of society. This theory was brilliantly presented by Malcom Gladwell in his book, *Outliers*. As individuals, though, we may have a different timing from that which is imposed by the school system, or by our parents' wishes. But if we do not kill our own potential by labeling ourselves useless, we can learn anything that is out there to be learned.

STOP TELLING YOURSELF LIES

Labeling ourselves as something unchangeable tends to convince us about that lie. You are not "poor" as an unchangeable trait that you were born with. You may be horribly broke, or you may have been involved in a long economical struggle, or you may have been born into poverty, but you are not poor as an unchangeable condition.

Once you comprehend that those limitations are nothing but the story you choose to create, or the absurd label that you have picked for yourself, the door you will open is phenomenally liberating. Then, you can embody change as a way to approach life.

So when we feel like we must take a major leap in our life, we need to listen to that call. We need to remind ourselves that we are actually malleable and capable of change, that most fixed traits are but a story—an idea—that we have created about ourselves.

Most of the time, this story of who we are and who we are not (these labels) come from one or two single traumatic moments in our childhood or adolescence.

So, being change is knowing that change is perfectly normal and feasible for you. In fact, it is a law of the universe, all you have to do is accept this fact.

But embodying change also takes practice. Practice means gaining awareness about our rigid areas, our patterns, and our habits, and

33

challenging them boldly. We do this by changing little things around us all the time and resisting becoming slaves to habits.

More profound ways to train yourself to be malleable to change is by living periods of your life in lifestyles that are as distant as possible from yours. Living in other cultures, visiting other religions, changing hobbies, undertaking sports, becoming interested in ways other people spend their lives, learning how they care for their children, observing how they care for their elderly, and so on. All of these ways to practice change are available to us. We will look deeper into this method further along in this book.

DRIVING YOUR OWN LIFE

As change is unescapable for us, we might as well try to give it direction.

Too often, the alternative to anticipating change and giving it direction is to allow all the complexity of life to push us randomly and crash us against a hard wall, time and time again.

The suggestion here is to not only to accept that there is an inevitability to change, but also to master its navigation while you travel inside this environment called life. Just like birds and planes use wind to their advantage—instead of fighting it—we can learn to navigate change.

Listen attentively to the wind of change when it starts to blow in your heart.

Being aware of and sensitive to your world is fundamental. If you do not evolve with your friends, you will eventually clash with them. The best way to keep long-term friendships is to grow together and not to expect things to remain frozen in time.

Life never stops changing and, if you can change more or less in harmony with life, you can avoid feeling like a branch planted in a tiny island fighting a storm in the middle of the ocean.

If you practice and become better at handling change, you could even find pleasure on that first day at the new job or at the new school. If you resist the unfamiliar at all costs, when an inevitable change in the workplace comes along, you will most likely feel at odds with your new environment. Adaptation will take longer and be painful.

We all must get out of our comfort zone in order to grow. We all should have well developed change antennas. We should always seek to continue changing inside and outside throughout life. But most importantly, we should know that we are capable of making fantastic changes in our own lives and behavior.

Today, we know more about our brains than ever before. For example, neuroscientist Michael Merzenich, professor emeritus at the University of California, San Francisco, and one of the foremost researchers of neuroplasticity today, is uncovering how we are in control of our mental abilities, and how they are capable of continuous modification and improvement. Merzenich's work demonstrates that the brain retains its ability to alter itself well into adulthood. Merzenich's fascinating work has shown how entire areas of the brain become totally remodeled and become specialized for the task at hand. Even in learning a simple skill, he reports, fifteen or twenty cortical areas are changed; this affects tens of millions, or even hundreds of millions of neurons in your brain.

Sadly, for many people, life begins with immense challenges such as a traumatic childhood impacted by violence or abuse, or the horrors of war, or by poverty, or by racism or any of many forms of human exploitation. Some people must learn to walk on a rocky trail, while others get a nice paved runway at the beginning of their life to take off and fly from. Escaping the trap of destiny is especially useful for those who are born in less-advantaged situations. Know that, you are able to get out of a life that feels like a train rushing toward a highly undesirable destination.

IMPORTANT AND URGENT

When a force inside you asks for change—whether that force expresses itself in the form of high stress, sadness, annoyance, frustration, anger, dislike for people around you or any other form—it is time to gather courage and dig inside yourself. It is time to find the part of your world that is out of harmony.

Do not neglect these forces inside you, because they can cause serious damage.

Change becomes more urgent when we are talking about unwanted situations that are sustained over time and that are also time intensive; this means those situations that are an integral part of your daily life. The most common ones are job and family.

Many are the reasons why different people neglect these internal calls, and we have a full chapter on anchors to change, but the point we need to stress here is the urgency to confront this kind of request from your heart.

Facing changes in integral parts of life is always more challenging. What I mean by "integral" here is the type of change that will affect your life in many dimensions. Divorce, for instance, can easily feel very threatening because it may imply changing homes, lifestyle, friends, economic status, and feeling lonely and judged. These changes can be harder than starting a new business in terms of energy output and emotional drain. And, that is one reason why people tend to neglect the signals and sweep them under the carpet without knowing that facing these changes is not only important, it is urgent. It has to be done.

The first task of acknowledging that you need to make a change is an important step, even if the actual execution of the change cannot be realized right away. The decision to move in a new direction must occur in your heart, followed by a strategy with steps along a path. I stress the importance of not procrastinating, and of having a genuine intention to change.

Do not let the pile of things that you need to tackle overwhelm you and keep you frozen in misery. No, emphatically no! Mountains are climbed one step at a time.

APPLYING THE CORRECT MEDICINE

Nothing should stop you from listening to your heart, nor from facing the fact that you need to be the master of your ship.

Now, once you have decided to do something about it, slow down. Search again and see that you are applying the correct medicine; that is, making the correct change.

For instance, change may not always entail leaving your job or leaving an entire way of life behind. A careful analysis will give you options, real options both in terms of total solutions as well as in terms of temporary or partial solutions. Sometimes very small changes inside you (such as a shift in viewpoint) can open huge doors to happier approaches to life.

Stagnation in a bad situation is never healthy. Being unhappy due to lack of our own action is a bit like drinking poisoned water by choice every day. Eventually it will take a toll on you. So, be fair to yourself and take action to produce a change that you know you need. It is the one decision that you do not want to postpone.

YOUR INTUITION MUSCLE

Learning to pay attention to our intuition is fundamental for becoming agile throughout life's changes.

We all have access to intuition. The difference between those more developed and less developed in this department lies in the degree of attention that one person pays to their intuition and trains that "intuition-reading muscle." Through practice, you can learn how to use your intuition more and more as you walk through life.

It is totally true that the voice of intuition can be confusing and even frustrating when something results in a fiasco, but learning to listen to yourself is worth the eventual frustrations.

Little by little, you will find yourself walking through life like the correct note of a melody. This should not be a privilege, but in our current increasingly distracting world, it is becoming a privilege. Our children are growing up with all the emphasis on their heads, while becoming truly numb to other inputs like intuition and emotional intelligence.

Much unhappiness in the world stems from people who shut their doors to what their heart is needing. Often expressed in the form of what we call intuition, what I am describing is the voice of your true self, your heart, your soul. The longer we ignore this part of us, the harder a cover we build to our ability to listen to our internal guiding system.

Closing the doors to our heart makes us lost wanderers in a sea of confusion, unsatisfied beings looking for answers in the wrong places. This is often expressed in the pursuance of money and accumulation of material wealth, to eventually die filthy rich and unhappy as ever. (Money is perfectly fine, when it comes as a byproduct of what makes you happy.)

THE ENGINE IS INSIDE

The universe is changing around you and certainly carrying you along, but the changes that have to do with your own life have a pilot.

It is you. It is your true self: that part of you capable of observing how you live your own life.

Let us not forget that we see the world through our very own personal lenses. These lenses have been built by our experiences and are modifiable. And, these lenses often do not even see reality as plain and simple as it is. We tint our reality with meaning and stories ruining our ability to experience life fully every moment. This is why we need constant work inside ourselves, in order to see the true colors of life.

Much of the fundamental change needed resides in our ability to see reality without preconceptions and biases. When we accomplish an unbiased view of life, our antennas become much more finely tuned. Finding the right note in the melody of your life will be easy and natural. Now you can catch the wind and ride it.

Attaining a clear view of life, however, is not easy. We are victims of much programming and a thick filter of preconceptions. Most human suffering comes from the added meaning that we attach to things that are otherwise neutral. Penetrating these filters that build up from traumatic events is a must in order to find happiness.

The good news is that becoming a person of change, a change ninja, will help you attain a clearer view of life—helping you leave behind filters and preconceptions that tie you down.

BE IN SHAPE: BIG CHANGE IS STRESSFUL

Being in harmony with your surroundings is not a just nice philosophical concept for Eastern books. Being in tune with our immediate world (our family, friends, city, career, potentialities, opportunities, risks, etcetera) is the way to finding good mental and emotional health.

Change is not easy, and because it is not easy, most people resist change and live very unfulfilling lives; sometimes, with horrible outcomes.

In physical human activity, being fit will always give you an advantage over those who have not trained or those who have sporadic activity. For those who train for 40K marathons, a 10K is a breeze.

The big difference is that when we talk about change and not marathons, change is not optional, marathons are. Life has already enrolled you for change the moment you were conceived inside your mother.

People who are used to change know how to gauge the stress that comes with different major moves. Prepare for a period of increased stress, and survive the surge that comes with major changes in life.

For someone who has never left his hometown and the only job he has had was at his grandparents' grocery store, the shock of the decision to move to a city can be unbearable: He must get a new job, with a new boss, with new rules, with new faces, within a new culture and in a city that is twenty times larger and three times as unsafe as his home town. Some practicing may be the right recipe for someone like this: This person might decide to take a class as a way to see new faces and meet new people. Also, small daily changes to existing routines might help this person—such as following different routes to work, changing dress style, or taking short trips every weekend.

Being a person fit for change will always give you an advantage to survive and thrive once you have gained mastery of the new situation. For example, undergoing a change of job will likely result in levels of stress that may make you cranky and irritable when you come home. Consequently, this may undermine relationships at home and create a domino effect that eventually could lead to a traumatic experience. On the other hand, a person who is fit for change will manage this kind of transition at work successfully without wreaking havoc at home.

The whole point here is to understand that the exercises that I will recommend to you below will be important. As your subconscious begins to understand that changes are normal, you will become fitter and fitter to change. Then, it will become easier, and that is when you will start to soar to new heights.

TIMING

When your heart cries for change, change is always healthy, but that same change performed with precise timing has multiplied powers.

As much as I stress not to procrastinate, I must also emphasize not to rush for change in a purely reactive manner. Timing is a beautiful skill in life and people with this skill perform major changes in their lives like music flowing from note to note.

Timing is also intuitive, so once again, stepping away from life's noise on a regular basis is a fundamental practice in order to capture the rhythm of your immediate world and therefore act with good timing.

In my practice with clients, I have noticed a very interesting connection; people who dance or practice martial arts tend to have good instinctive timing that somehow transcends the physical body and gives them good radar for general timing in their life.

In any case, timing is also learning to breathe once before you react out of anger or pressure. Learn to say "let me sleep on it," and truly do so.

Neal Cabage, a leader in digital product strategy, provides us some strong examples of the value of timing in business decisions. He points out how Apple's app store became a good opportunity for developers who could create interactive content. Today, more than half a million apps are available, but fifty percent of the revenue is generated by only twenty-five developers. Cabage also points out how innovation was not necessarily the first ingredient to success but, rather, it was timing: Google did not invent the search engine. Facebook did not invent the social network, and Yelp did not invent online reviews.

INTEGRITY AND YOUR CORE VALUES

Whether we actually change our core values through life or they remain the same as part of the essence of who we really are, I do not know. I can only speak from my own life experience.

Although my views and opinions on many things have changed over life, I feel that some core values inside still feel very comfortably in place and they seem to be unchangeable. I do not imagine ever believing that abuse of power is acceptable or that torture is okay, just to mention two examples.

Thus, all this conversation about the benefits of our being creatures capable of understanding the importance of change and of developing the ability to pilot change in our own lives requires a very important clarification: Changing your core principles at a given moment due to pressure or convenience is not the change that we are talking about here. Changing your values about corruption when you are offered a bribe is not the kind of change I encourage.

Just to pick one immediate example, we all witness rampant lack of integrity every day when some people who have made huge amounts of money in business still desperately invest money into corrupting the souls of public servants. No matter that these public servants have been put into positions of power by the trust and hope of their electors. And then, we often watch these elected officials, who once promised to be honest, crumble to dust before our very eyes once they compromise themselves for money or power.

We can easily witness how greed for money or position so effortlessly changes people's stances—often publicly and with apparently no shame. Or even in spite of shame. This is not the change I suggest here.

A STORY ABOUT INTEGRITY

We clearly know when we are betraying ourselves. Even in extreme situations when our life is on the line, we know what is right and what is wrong in relation to our own moral compass. We know when we sell our integrity to save our neck.

I have a breathtaking example of integrity evinced by the man with the highest degree of this trait whom I have met thus far in my life. He happens to be my late father. He spent his youth and early adult years in an era of great political unrest and recurring coups d'etat and revolutions typical of a small country. Bolivia changed governments about once a year on average in those times. As a university student, my father had participated in at least one revolution against the also commonly abusive regimes. Guns of all sorts were typical in any home.

One day when protestors had been reacting to a failed coup d'etat where the leader had been arrested and was being held in a police compound, my father and his friend (the one who told me the story more than forty years later) were walking near the capital's central square minding their own business. The city's main square is where the presidential palace is located.

An agitated crowd of about one hundred caught their attention in one of the corners of the square. My father and his friend approached to discover that this enraged group of men and women were holding a man—the failed coup leader—who had been yanked out of the police compound by this mob. What the two young men saw was a shocking lynching scene.

German E. Velasco

The mob's prisoner was disfigured, covered in blood, with open wounds visible in face and head. Both eyes were bleeding as he begged the mob to kill him out of mercy. The mob would not stop kicking and whipping him with belts, ropes and wooden sticks. A small group was preparing a rope to hang the badly injured man. My father and his friend watched horrified, not knowing what to do.

Once the crowd was able to ready the rope, they proceeded to hang the poor wretch. The makeshift gallows failed as the rope broke. The man fell to the granite pavement getting hurt even worse.

My young father intervened and tried to talk to the mob, reminding them that it is customary to spare the person's life when the rope breaks, (an unwritten agreement anywhere where someone is to die by hanging). The mob ignored the plea of my father and his friend. The rope was repaired and a second attempt was made. The rope broke again and the victim of the mob fell again hitting face and body on the hard ground. More kicks, more hits with sticks and belts.

My father and friend made a new attempt to talk to the crowd given that the rope had broken twice. The crowd remained determined to hang the man. The man continued to scream in pain and asked to be put to death at once. A group headed off to find a better rope.

My dad's friend whispered into my dad's ear, "I have a gun but I do not dare." My young father told his friend, "Give me your gun." Then, this courageous man of unbreakable integrity put a bullet in the man's head and ended his life.

A newspaper article described the incident the next day. The article ended with the phrase "…an angel's hand put an end to his suffering."

However distasteful and unnatural the act, my father was willing to end a man's life in order to spare him from suffering. Flow with change but keep your integrity.

7
ENJOYING YOUR WINGS

If you are one of those lucky people who from a young age naturally liked change, sought out change and had that urge to explore beyond your tiny immediate world, you can probably easily contribute to the list of ideas I am about to present in this chapter.

Learning to like change and promoting it in your life is like an ever unfolding multidirectional flower with multiple benefits in several directions. Here are some benefits I have discovered in my observations of strangers who seem to have the knack for change, and also from my clients who have embodied change, and from my own direct experience with change.

LIVING MULTIPLE LIFETIMES

If you are one of those people who has changed career one or two or three times, you know how it feels to live two or three lifetimes.

Reading about the life of a truck driver is different than living the life of a truck driver. Reading about what Doctors Without Borders do around the world is one thing; living the experience is another.

Most people do not realize they have everything in their hands to make a shift and experience a much richer life. A richer life happens when you fully experience a different lifestyle. A different culture, or a different career, or both at once will give you the experience of having lived two separate lifetimes, and you can carry the experience from one lifetime to the other.

A dentist who works for forty years in his same dental office, about ten hours per day, treating similar cases, of the same patients (and then their children) is a person who involuntarily cultivates rigidity to change and at the same time lives in a groove, perhaps aware that there is a world out there, but not living it. This is a person who misses out on the diversity that this world offers.

If you are a person who wants to stick to one career throughout your life it better be for the love of it, but you should always find ways to evolve within that career—and hopefully explore other areas of life, such as culture, language, geography.

A person living in the habit of habits in a routine of routines is a person who deprives himself from the opportunity to savor life. What would you say about a friend who as a rule, would eat only one kind of fruit, orange, and refused to try any other fruit? We do something similar when we accept a linear life and we do not embody change.

If you ride the same bus to work every day for several months, unless you make a specific conscious effort to be present every time you travel in that bus, chances are you will be repeating your first ride over and over again. But if instead, every time you board the bus you are fully aware that the entire universe has moved since the last time you took a similar bus, you will be open to the incredible adventure that life offers all the time.

As a quick exercise, let us compare person A, ten hour per day job for ten years, versus person B, moving two years to Africa, and then living three years in Japan, and then working two years in Alaska, and then founding a touring company in Baja, California. We cannot help but see one person as having wings and the other one as having chains.

> "Wealth is the ability to fully experience life." Henry David Thoreau

CREATIVITY

Arguably number one on my list of ways to enjoy being a change-ninja is creativity. Creativity is a quality of the adventurer and also the quality of the genius. Creativity is either born with the person or grows in the individual who strives to pursue it.

Creativity requires the mindset that something different is always possible and that something new is always waiting around the corner and all you have to do is keep walking and you will find it. Steve Jobs, the co-founder of Apple, is another great contemporary example of a change-ninja. His creativity and resourcefulness influenced entire industries, transforming them from the previous way that the world had perceived them: computers, movies, retail sales, music, phones, tablets, and digital publishing.

But for creativity to be unleashed, the person has to become comfortable with change, and has to win over fears and anchors that keep him or her tied to a rock. (Some people are highly creative and they do not know it because they are afraid of change.)

When we stop and really look at what creativity truly does in a person's life and the potential that this quality has for the world, it is like an expanding cloud. Creativity can permeate every area of existence because it is applicable to every area of one's life.

Creative people are hardly ever bored. When bored they daydream, and they create. They tend to live exciting lives because they are explorers by nature. Creative people may age but they never truly get old; they are too busy being fascinated with life in all of its dimensions.

I am not the only one who connects creativity to the ability to manage change easily. If we read psychologist Mihaly Csikszentmihalyi who has studied creative types for over thirty years, he says:

Creative individuals are remarkable for their ability to adapt to almost any situation and to make do with whatever is at hand to reach their goals. If I had to express in one word what makes their personalities different from others, it is complexity. They show tendencies of thought and action that in most people are segregated. They contain contradictory extremes; instead of being an 'individual', each of them is a 'multitude.'

But even more interestingly, creative people also create the possibility for something new in their lives time and time again. They intuitively know how to build the next portion of the bridge that will eventually cross the river.

This is perhaps the greatest tool that a human being could ask for if given one choice while left in a wilderness. Creativity would probably provide the best possibilities of survival.

For the creative person there is always a possibility. For the rigid of mind, the first obstacle can turn into an impassable barrier.

Hence, I make the strong recommendation to exercise both hemispheres of your brain. Further along in this book, I will provide you with concrete exercises for doing so. Seek to become a creative type. Life is fuller, more colorful, and full of challenges that are tackled with delight.

FREEDOM

Most of the things that restrain our freedom live inside us, in our personal view of life or in what some call a model of the world. Our beliefs, our traumatic experiences, our biases, our stories created and believed as true, our fear of the unfamiliar and many other things along those lines are truly our own worse slave drivers.

The connection is clear: The moment we realize that our life is not mounted on a rail with one fixed direction but rather flying on wings like a bird that can change direction any time, according to desires, needs or environmental situations, we are freer by definition. If we add freedom of choice at its most practical level, such as intrinsically knowing that you are not condemned to your career, your job, or a toxic relationship, the contrast in levels of freedom between rigid people and change-ninjas begins to be dramatic.

Another huge area where change-ninjas gain freedom lies in being able to leave the past behind. Why is this easier for them? Because of a basic principle. People who embody change know that the direction is forward, they are optimistic about the next turn, and therefore they leave the past behind much more easily than rigid types.

The ability to change with new situations and to adapt, includes a long list of typical things that are inevitably painful in life, like heartbreak, like losing a loved one, having to leave your home and country, getting separated from your family, and so on. For all these, I am sure there are many remedies available, but one certain booster is to be good at change. Bad things happen in life; knowing how to come to terms with them may require some skills not related to change, but knowing how to move out of situation A to situation B will always help immensely.

THE CHOICE TO REACT

Everything that tends to make us rigid to change is a sabotage against our freedom at our innermost essential level. One surprising blind spot that affects millions of people is owning the choice of how to react. Living a linear life in a groove nullifies our freedom to choose a reaction to whatever life throws at us.

If we imagine a good soccer goalie, what makes him or her invincible is the ability to make the right move in reference to the nearest context. The goalie has no control over the entire context of the game until a shot is coming toward his goal. Then he acts. Some choices may be:

1. He may stand and watch the ball fly into the net.
2. He may lunge and catch the ball.
3. He may lunge, miss and fail at stopping the ball.

People who are rigid to change tend to have one way and only one way to catch the ball. Sometimes it works, but most of the time it does not. And likely, they adopted that one approach because it worked once. They spend the rest of their lives hoping that the approach works again.

It is not over. Our goalie has many more options:

4. He may sit in place and cry.
5. He may curse and walk out of the field and quit for good.
6. He may get up and keep playing with a loser's attitude, feeling like a total failure.
7. He may get up and keep playing having learned one more thing from his recent failure and feeling an ounce more expert.

You get the point. You can probably think of many more things the goalie could do. If that goalie has such a diverse palette of options, imagen a comment from your boss instead of that soccer ball, or a comment from your partner. The options at your disposal are many, some extremely constructive and some extremely destructive. It is your choice.

When someone willingly or unwillingly hurts us, the shot has been fired. How to deal and heal is our option. One person may choose to cling to hate and revenge against the shooter for the next twenty years while another may decide to end that relationship, create some distance, make an effort to understand what happened and let go of all ill feelings as quickly as possible.

People who are agile at change are good at creating new options to react, more in tune with the moment, and respond more appropriately to the specific challenge.

HEALTH

When we suppress our emotions and feelings, we do not do well. Pretty much all medical opinion now agrees that the emotional will manifest physically sooner or later. Now think of the potential damage that you can cause to yourself when you spend long periods of time thirsty for change in your life, feeling trapped in a situation.

Having the courage to move out of an unwanted place, whether it is a bad relationship or a job, is absolutely worth it for all the reasons we have been listing, but also for your physical health.

Developing a sense of your inner boundaries is a great tool for living in a healthy relationship with the world. When something feels like a constant menace to your boundaries it is time to take action. Staying in a place where your boundaries are constantly violated is a sure path to emotional and physical problems.

Practicing change in small things is a way to teach your subconscious that change is possible, and it keeps you from becoming rigid to change when a situation has turned into a real threat to your health.

OPTIMISM AND RESOURCEFULNESS

I want to put these two attributes together because in my experience they tend to go hand in hand. Optimists tend to be the ones who find new resources because they do not give up easily. Resourceful people are optimistic because they are used to finding options to solve problems.

Throughout my life I have discovered that those who know me see me as a resourceful person. I am the "there's got to be a way" guy.

As a norm, I take the obstacle as a challenge and hardly ever as an impassable wall. I have a little story to illustrate this point.

Many years ago I was traveling in a Toyota SUV with a film production crew in a remote road in southern Bolivia. As in most of Bolivia, this was a very mountainous terrain. Suddenly we spotted a long line of stopped cars going in our same direction. No traffic was coming from the opposite direction. We got out of the car to investigate what was holding up all these travelers, and we discovered that there were some one-hundred fifty cars standing ahead of us. People were picnicking, relaxing and playing cards. This was not an encouraging sight for those of us who were running on a tight schedule. There had been a collision of two trucks, and one of them blocked the road. We were told that a tow truck was coming, and we knew that the soonest it could arrive would be five or six hours.

My first thought was that there had to be a simple alternate route around the small town that sat hanging from the hill on both sides of the road. But something also told me that those people were patiently waiting for a good reason and I was just being an impatient fool. Nevertheless, I asked a couple of members of my crew to help me take measurements of the width of our SUV. Next, we walked along a possible route, a combination of steep inclined terrain, stairs and more stairs, and cobblestone and dirt with narrow pedestrian streets.

We took rapid inventory of potential obstacles and thought about on-the-spot solutions. We laid out a few rocks and logs to lessen the height of the steps. Our scouting ended at the other side of town with a four-hundred-step climb—steep, pyramid style. After that, we came across a couple of basketball courts and eventually the highway!! As you can imagine, we pulled the SUV out from the long line in front of hundreds of wondering eyes. We succeeded in our little adventure and we said goodbye to the crowd. I am sure many followed our route.

Optimism at its most practical level is characteristic of resourceful people. "There's always a way."

I am sure I owe much of my resourcefulness to having spent my childhood in a poor Third World country right before television arrived. Although we were not poor, I had many friends that made their own toys and we had to find fun and entertainment in the most improbable resources. Watching the resilience of the poor is like stepping into a different world.

GETTING PAST YOUR PAST

People who are change-ninjas have less difficulty than others at letting go of a traumatic experience in their past. Change-friendly people understand at a deep, intuitive level that the past resides in the past, and although a traumatic experience may show up as new threat in the future, making the distinction is easier for them.

There are plenty of professionals who offer specific help in healing trauma. My first advice here is to not hesitate and seek professional help if you have issues with past trauma. It is never too soon to gain freedom from the past. Your therapist will likely agree that exercising change in your life can only help accelerate your healing immensely.

The change-ninja will shake off past burdens and free himself from what seems a life with one door and one lock.

On the opposite side, there is an inherent serious disadvantage for rigid people when it comes to letting go of the past. Even when rigid people finally drag themselves to find a solution to a problem, they tend to hold on to it as the only medicine and if the problem changes a little, the solution does not work anymore. Yet, people with a rigid approach to life tend to keep trying endlessly to apply that one solution, "the proven one." The treasure is gone, yet we keep coming back to that place where we once found it.

People who flow with life will leave that past solution to the past problem in the past, trusting that new problems will call for new solutions, and the pool of possible solutions is endless. (At least as large as the possibility of new challenges.)

For the change-ninja, a new experience is a new experience, not a repetition of the past. The past does not exist to a person of change. To the rigid at heart, the past will never be over, and that's a waste of a life.

Among my clients, I often find the most suffering and pain in people who keep living in the past. To live in the past, you do not need to be insane or stupid. We all tend to do it when we ask "why did it have to happen" or "I wish I had done things differently" or "I wish I had read the signs" or "we should have done this or that." The kind of thoughts that include a wish that we could change the past are precisiely what keep us in the past. The kind of thought that says "there is nothing I can do about it, and what is the best next step?" is the kind of liberating thought we need to move forward with.

Because it is so common, divorce is one of the most underestimated traumatic experiences in our society. We know a death or a disaster is supposed to be shocking, but we do not expect to be shocked by the most hopeful and delightful experience: falling in love with and marrying someone.

If we were to observe in a laboratory how most relationships begin and fast-forward to a divorce, we would very clearly conclude that divorce is a shocking phenomenon to any system. It is not in the range of normal things we expect from life to happen to us. It also carries with it a significant number of reasons to keep us in the past: How nice it used to be. When did it change? Why did it change? Is it my fault? Is it my partner's fault? What if I had done this or that differently? Etcetera.

Freedom from the past often comes when a person simply shifts a tiny angle in his point of view. First, accepting that this is a new reality because life changes. Second, acceptance that there is nothing wrong with still loving the person that you are divorcing. Third, not attaching any expectation to your love for someone. (Certainly do not attach the belief that because you love the other person, this divorce should not happen.)

Being able to leave the past behind has many, many more positive applications that result in expanding your overall freedom. Some of those applications make a life-changing difference. Another example I observe in divorce coaching is anger and/or resentment. The longer you keep your grudges, the longer you are turning over your freedom to the hands of the wrong person—the person you dislike or hate. Grudges are self-imposed chains.

RELATIONSHIPS, LOVE AND HEARTBREAK

If you are able to love, consider yourself lucky. Feeling true love is a privilege.

Love, this big thing that seems capable of performing miracles, has no purpose other than allowing you to feel the biggest, most fascinating of all human emotions. Period. Love is that, and that is quite a treat in itself.

What we decide to do once we have that feeling inside is a whole other thing.

Loving another being does not require anything—just for love to exist inside you. It exists because you allow it to exist. Love exists inside you, nowhere else. And even though you are only a few feet tall, a few inches wide and deep, the love that lives inside you may very well occupy several square miles. Love is a big thing.

Changes in life that have to do with this powerful feeling can be overwhelmingly large too. Yes, unfortunately, life is not perfect. In order to feel love, you must become vulnerable.

Since life is about changes, at some point, very likely, we will have to say goodbye to that being who has been with us forever. His or her departure will bring pain indescribably intense, overwhelming and sharp. There is hardly any protection for that, other than knowing ahead of time that nothing is permanent and that when that person leaves there will be pain. It will throw you on the hard cement and will make you cry. And then cry some more.

But the good news is that protection exists against other aspects of heartbreak. Namely, understanding true love and touching its true nature may help ease pain when undergoing heartbreak.

Going through a heartbreaking experience is devastating for most people. But, as we been pondering since the beginning of this book, much of our being more or less happy in life hinges on our approach to life—on our view and model of the world. And in my opinion, having a true understanding of love will help protect many people from unnecessary pain and suffering.

I am convinced—by having coached literally hundreds of people through divorce—that nothing has as much protective power as a true understanding of what this feeling called love is.

Developing the skill to separate certain beliefs that do not belong together helps us understand love in its real dimension.

Our greatest confusion, which is an open invitation to pain, is our expectation that because I love a person, that person must love me in return, or else my love is "incomplete." Or even worse: if that person does not love me in return for my love, that person is not worthy of my love. All the expectations and beliefs about what should happen as a consequence of feeling love for someone do not belong in the same box as love. Your love for someone belongs alone in one box, bag, shelf. (Pick the metaphor that works for you.)

Another simple yet powerful assumption is that because I love you, you must be my partner, the mother of my children, my moral support and everything else I need. Wrong assumption. Love is a one-way feeling and it is not attached to any form of partnership of any sort.

The person you love is not supposed to be the filler of your voids. He or she is not a cork or a patch or a bandage. Learn to love without expecting anything in return and you will be a free person.

Love is not a preamble into something else. Nothing is supposed to happen as a mandatory chapter two. Something may happen in connection with this love or nothing may happen in connection with this love that you feel. And if it exists in you, you are very lucky because you are experiencing the most glorious feeling people can grasp.

When someone else happens to feel true love for you, consider yourself twice as privileged.

Most of the heartbreak I have seen emerges from a deep misunderstanding that contaminates love with a form of ownership. True love only flows out from you.

Many millions and millions of people have the double privilege of loving and being loved by a partner. But I am sure that just as many other millions have the purest form of love in their hearts for a person who is not a partner of any sort, and they understand that nothing is to be expected. Love exists in them. Life is good.

Lots and lots of soap opera, brainwashing drama has programmed this false conception in us: If she does not love me, she may qualify as my enemy, a target of my rage. Thousands of stories in the fictional world have become real stories where the person who is not loved devotes his or her life to taking revenge against the one who dared to not love him back.

True love is the most outstanding and greatest feeling that can inhabit any human heart; consequently, when we misunderstand this feeling, we miss out on the best thing that life has to offer. Yes, the misunderstanding of this fundamental feeling (precisely because it is so fundamental to human beings and requires opening the heart to vulnerability) can lead to profound and devastating effects.

RICH, EXTENDED LIFE

Other benefits I have consistently observed in people who are agile at change are extended active and fulfilling lives.

The formula for these successes is quite simple: As time goes by, the change-ninjas get richer and richer in skills in a number of ways. As they approach a stage when some activities are not possible anymore, they have a palette of options, be it painting, piano, writing or teaching. The list can be very long.

One of my most inspiring friends today is Ruth Wright, the original advocate and activist who influenced the adoption of key environmental policies in Boulder, Colorado about forty years ago. Ruth is eighty-eight years old today and she is extremely busy investing her lucid mind fighting new fights in environmental policy elsewhere. Over the years she has gotten a law degree, written books, including writing the best-selling guide to Machu Picchu in Peru. When it is time to move to a completely new project, Ruth just does it. Her past endeavors go to strengthen the richness of her life. They are never an anchor.

Our misunderstanding concerning richness versus material wealth can play a mean trick on us when we realize that millions of dollars in the bank are worth nothing once we have lived forty or fifty years devoted only to accumulating dollar bills. True wealth comes from living a fulfilling life by riding through intense sad moments, and enjoying the depths of many happy moments.

The enjoyment of old age is also a function of flexibility and adaptation to change. I have a not-so-happy example observing my mother's path of aging.

MY MOM'S THIRTY-YEAR MISCALCULATION

My mother, ninety-two at the time that this book is being written, declared herself "old" about thirty years ago and she has become increasingly bored in her big house over the past three decades. She was a person devoted to keeping her house impeccable and pretty. But she was not a person of change. If she were, she would have picked up new skills, passions, and hobbies with the passing of the years, but she was too set on her ways. Her health was impeccable thirty years ago.

Ever since I can remember, Mom always woke up at the same time, and took a shower always at the same time (even in her worst days of having a cold). Then she started with her day of housework. She had a specific routine; she always started at the same end of the house and finished in the other end. Monday was floor-waxing day and Friday was market day. Every day of the week had a specific meal. My mother has been a rigid person, and she has been having a hellish time adapting to life without my father over the last three years.

My father, on the other hand, passed away at ninety-two and still had to sign some checks and letters for his business the next day. At ninety-two, Dad ran his business remotely from home, part-time. He remained active to his last day. He never devoted time to waiting for death, he just kept going. My father was much more flexible and malleable to changes than my mother.

The point is that when we reach a certain age, having been a change-ninja comes in handy.

My mother's story is far more relevant now to the new generations who have gained precisely those extra thirty years of potentially active life!

Plan for it, live it, and squeeze the most out it.

German E. Velasco

BEFRIEND COMPUTERS

The single most important change I strongly recommend to every adult who still resists computer technology is to befriend these machines.

A handful of inventions have provided humanity with an extraordinary opportunity to enjoy those golden years like never before. At least they have given us a fantastic window to the world and a means to communicate in this era when the elderly are not in touch with their children and grandchildren on a daily basis.

Computers, software and internet have transformed our world and this transformation fits people who are physically less active like a glove. Nobody should get to age eighty without having mastered the basic computer technology available today.

Being able to see your loved ones and converse with them in real time while being thousands of miles away is a luxury that did not cross our ancestors' minds in their wildest dreams.

Or take FaceBook for example; what an extraordinary tool to keep in touch in real time with friends that may have scattered all over the map over several decades. And, it is all perfectly democratized because it is free.

The elderly do not have to be isolated waiting for the postman to bring a letter like my parents did when I went away to college. A device with internet capabilities should be a human right—especially for older people.

But communications is not the only reason for adults to learn computing now! Another reason is the productivity that you can squeeze out of these machines at any age. Whether for entertainment or to produce something for the world, computers are where the action will be. We just need to be open to change and that means being willing to learn more and more as times moves through us and with us.

8

ANCHORS THAT PREVENT CHANGE

Even when we want to change a situation in our lives and we are committed to changing it, as undesirable as our current situation may be, part of us still resists change.

Familiarity is quite a drug for us humans; we like it more than we imagine. The comfort found in the familiar also affects our biases and fuels our imagination, creating stories that often rule our lives. Most of our biases and preconceptions about the unfamiliar face, place or behavior emerges from this tiny place that feels familiar.

As we discussed before, moving out of the little hole where we live in a familiar space (sometimes an ugly dark hole) is a step to begin growing wings. Getting out, learning that it is possible, and doing it again and again eventually changes the quality of life radically.

Finding our anchors to healthy change is vital for a full, rich life. Let's summarize some common anchors that keep people stuck in life.

WHO YOU ARE AND WHO YOU ARE NOT

As discussed, a very common anchor is to believe that we are what we do. "Mr. Jones is a mechanic." "I am an architect." The labeling that we receive or that we place upon ourselves is no small anchor. At the very least, we should make an inward effort to recognize, very clearly, the difference between being and doing whatever we do for a living.

We are not our profession. We are not our activity. We are beings who far transcend the relative smallness of a degree or a tittle.

Another underlying reason as to why we may "become" our profession is the sweat and tears we often invest in attaining one. Attaining a college degree is hard and we often feel that not labeling ourselves as being that is a sacrilege.

It is not a sacrilege. There are social recognitions accorded to many professions in a given society. It is nice for the ego to be treated somewhat differently because you carry a positively recognized label; and you can continue enjoying all prestige, but do not believe that you have become your skills. Do not make them your identity. Keep your freedom; do not chain yourself.

WEAR YOUR ROLE LIKE A COAT

I like to think of roles in society as things you wear for a given period of time and—at will—you can hang in a special closet. Think of your profession as a valuable coat that you can save in a safe place inside you.

You may decide to keep your profession or activity for many years or for life; that's just fine. What we are talking about here is subtle yet determinant: It all depends on the conception of yourself inside you. When people see themselves as what they do it becomes an overpowering anchor to freedom. It narrows the vision of life to a thin line called "profession."

Public office is a good school for learning how not to become the label that society has placed on you. Stepping down from high ranking offices such as President or Governor often carries people directly to the therapist. The loss of identity can be dramatic after leaving office, but only if the person has believed the lie that he was that title. The psychological power of a title can be impressive.

Some important writers come to mind relative to this concept of wearing your role like a coat: American novelist and journalist Jack

London traveled the seas as a sailor looking for subjects to write about; Alvin Toffler decided to work for years as a factory worker in order to study and write about mass production; Nobel Prize winner John Steinbeck wrote many of the greatest American novels seeking inspiration as an actual farm worker picking grapes with migrants in his native California.

REMOVING THE COAT

Working with visualization is most valid and surprisingly liberating: By finding a quiet setting and relaxing your body, you may imagine physically removing a coat, folding it, carrying it away and placing it on a nice clean shelf that is also a part of you. You can use the coat any time you want. It belongs only to you. No one else has access to that precious part of you. It is safe.

Feel the freedom. Visualize yourself lighter, ready to move towards a new space… unknown but shiny, bright, happier, attractive and warm.

This is the kind of exercise that allows you to create a new realm of possibilities. We will discuss the process of visualization in greater depth in a later section of this book, the Magic tower.

CREATE A COAT WHEN YOU NEED IT

Several studies point out that people tend to perform better when they see themselves as "being" something. For example, if you consider yourself a good golfer, you have higher chances of actually performing better than if you consider yourself a poor golfer.

So, why not use this trick? It is an exercise of visualization in order to convince yourself about how good you have become at your new ability.

Along this line, I encourage you to watch Amy Cuddy's Ted Talk to discover something even more interesting: How body language affects how others see us, and how it may also change how we see ourselves.

FORREST GUMP'S KEY TO SUCCESS

When I watch this story of a slow-witted boy who has never seen himself as disadvantaged, I see the wings of the person who has no preconceptions about what he or she can or cannot do. The movie is a beautiful illustration of what a life could be if there are no self-imposed boundaries. In the story, Forrest Gump wears the coat that he chooses and embodies that coat—until he decides to wear a different one.

BAD SELF-LABELING

"I am not a good at drawing." "I am not good at math." When we tell ourselves what we are or what we are not, we, quite literally, lock the door to changing such self-declared statuses. Treating the absence of certain skills at a given moment as a fixed trait is not good because it is not real.

Referring to ourselves as not being good at something is similar to seeing ourselves as an object that was manufactured for a single purpose: I am a toothbrush, therefore I cannot write on a piece of paper because I am not a pen. If people were born like appliances, then yes, it would be a huge waste of energy for a toaster to try to behave like a bicycle.

For the flexible mindset of a change-ninja, most things out there are open paths to an interesting challenge. For the rigid of mind, new things out there are seen as doors with combination locks that are likely very hard or impossible to open.

LANGUAGE AND SELF-LABELING

When we refer to ourselves as being something, we are attaching that something to our identity. We are telling ourselves a story that is not only not true, but is also a very bad recipe for our basic freedom.

There is a feature of language in the English language that should make us extra aware and careful about not adopting stories about what we are. The verb, "to be," can add permanence to situations that are not always ideal to accept as permanent.

"I am waiting for the bus" is very clearly implicitly temporary, because whether you say it in Spanish or English at the bus stop, there is no room for confusion. Again, it is temporary.

On the other hand, "I am poor" has a much heavier connotation in English, because if runs the risk of creating a belief about "who I am" as a permanent trait. So, if you have bought the belief that you are poor, how in the world could the same you ever become not poor?

In the Spanish language, by contrast, to express the status of being temporarily poor, you can use the same verb that you use to describe the waiting for the bus status, which is intrinsically temporary: *Estoy pobre*. Or, you may use the Spanish form of "to be" that describes intrinsic permanence: *Soy pobre*. Saying "soy pobre" has the same locking effect as in English. If a Spanish speaker chooses this form of expression, there is no room for confusion; he knows he is labeling himself as poor as a permanent trait.

This opens up a necessary discussion about beliefs, their power and their emptiness as well. Let's discuss that.

COMMITMENT TO BELIEFS

What we have just described is a form of commitment to a belief. It illustrates the power of a belief once we have accepted the story behind it. In this instance, the belief comes from repeated self-labeling. But many other limiting beliefs come from outside ourselves. First, let's consider what believing truly is and what kind of relevance we should give this notion in our lives.

The subject of beliefs may deserve an entire book, but for our purposes, let's briefly analyze this state of mind called believing. To begin, I think that there is room for confusion in the usage and meaning of this term in our day-to-day life. Let's explore the use of the word:

- I believe my brother is a good doctor. (I am convinced that my brother is a good doctor.)
- I believe in God. (I hold this idea as true.)
- I believe you when you say you went to the movies last night. (I accept your story as true.)
- I believe that one day we will go to Mars and live there. (I am convinced that the future will look as I imagine it now.)

In all the statements above, I want you to notice how irrelevant "believing" is to what actually occurs in reality. Whether I believe it or not:

- My brother would still be the same doctor that he is and has been.
- God would continue to exist or not exist regardless of my believing.
- If the person lied to me about being at the movies last night, my believing would not change where the person was.

There is an additional use that our culture sells us quite often: Believe it is possible and it will become real. Try believing really hard right now that you will find a million dollars in your closet next to your socks and please write me quickly if it happens. It won't. Life does not work like that.

Beliefs are only that. And I do not want to take away the relative value of believing that you can accomplish something versus believing the opposite. But the point is that assigning so much power to believing is not a good way to flow with reality. Here is why: Believing can become an anchor when we conceive that things are possible only when we believe they can exist.

The good news is that reality exists independently of whether we believe it exists or not.

Faith may be a good carrot to get us moving, but faith or believing is not a requirement to accomplish things in your life. Staying aware of your powers and your freedom: that is true powerful help. And then, as we discussed before, committing to beliefs is definitely chaining ourselves to a rock.

Devote some time to working on those beliefs you have created that limit your powers, and remember that beliefs are only beliefs... Move them out of your way.

THE PERSEVERANCE ANCHOR

Most of us are drilled with the value of perseverance in our lives. Not a bad thing. Not a good thing either. Perseverance is neutral; you can use this ability to your advantage or to your disadvantage. Just like you can use the kitchen knife to slice the bread that feeds your family, or you can use it to hurt yourself.

Yes, it is extremely important to be consistent and exercise perseverance while your objective is still calling you. On the other hand, it is not clever to be perseverant just for the sake of obsessively complying with your perseverance programming. This behavior can act as an anchor to necessary change.

For example, if a person discovers that his profession is not really what he wants to continue doing, yet he feels the obligation to persevere because he has twenty years invested in the field, that is a bad use of perseverance.

It is never too early to jump out of the train that is taking you to the wrong destination.

Some of my friends could not understand why I was happily supportive of my son's decision, that I have shared with you, to refuse a quarter-million-dollar scholarship for a Ph.D. when he decided he had had enough of that career. A year later he was getting his first job a computer programmer, and he was happy and fulfilled. Had he persevered in the path to his Ph.D., he would be one unhappy person with an impressive paper on the wall.

THE SOCIAL LIFE ANCHOR

Often our work world becomes our social life. This is another feeling that can give us a sense of commitment; in this case, to a group of people. The idea of leaving a workplace can legitimately generate a sense of loss, and that sense can be very real. Changing jobs sometimes means changing social worlds. This is a cost only you can assess.

Needless to say, this can vary between situations greatly. One approach to making a decision is to put this feeling on the table and weigh it with open self-honesty. How much of a priority is it to preserve this social world? Are there other strategic ways to preserve your friends and change work? Or, will you finally have to accept a loss in return for a greater gain?

Also consider other possible solutions to the specific problem. I guarantee you that you will find more than one strategy to attack the potential problem and resolve it.

It is always healthy to see the problem as it is. Denying that your social life is acting as your anchor will not help. Once you pinpoint your anchor, you will find a solution or a place in your heart to weigh your cost of moving forward.

THE HARD WORK ANCHOR

Again, I have nothing against hard work. I have nothing for hard work either, as it is a neutral tool. It can be used in your favor or to your detriment.

You could be digging the deepest tunnel towards the center of the earth and spend your life time working very hard, or you could spend time working hard for hours, months and years developing the most fuel-efficient airplanes for humanity. Both are hard work.

If you have become used to working hard as if by command from heaven and as a way to avoid guilt, please stop. Stop and see if you have not fallen into the hole we mentioned above, digging uselessly and wasting precious time that you could be spending with your loved ones.

Working extra hard generally means working longer days and weekends. It is always important to create some distance to assess why you are working hard. Working hard is, to a surprising degree, a way of avoiding situations that are begging for change in people's lives.

Working extra-long hours and weeks also gnaws away at our critical and analytic thinking time. This is the time we need to step outside of the forest of confusion and consider our life from a broader perspective. Some people never create the moment to see their lives from a distance and to make important discoveries—such as the fact they need a new job.

LOYALTIES AND LOYALTIES

Closely related to an overrated interpretation of belief is a misinterpreted loyalty.

I must start, however, by clarifying that true loyalty and integrity are not being questioned here. Not at all. These are fundamental qualities of the human race. These are the kind of values that should not to be compromised as long as they inhabit your own heart at any given moment and place.

What I wish to call into question here is a common misinterpretation of what loyalty should be. Yes, there is a gigantic difference between exercising loyalty to something by choice versus being loyal to something because you have mistakenly made it part of your identity.

This is one of those anchors that invisibly but effectively kill our ability to fly. The moment we tell ourselves that we are something that we empathize with or like, we are embarking in the wrong boat toward our freedom. We are never our loyalties; rather, we exercise our loyalties.

We should keep our loyalties while they still make complete sense within our value system. In other words, our commitment and allegiance should never be a blank check. For instance, the very instant that we remain loyal to an ideology that has failed us, we have lost an important part of our freedom. It is like having an extra chain that we absolutely do not need.

These are generally loyalties that we develop out of a need to belong and/or out of an urge to attach to what has become familiar to us. Or even worse, we become useful fools—militant members of ideas, trends, or notions—as we forget to question if these concepts still deserve our loyalty from one moment to the next.

Invitations to gain our loyalties often come packaged in a belief system that tricks us into actually believing that we are it. Once we have crossed the line of becoming, we have lost essential freedom to live our life the way we deserve.

"I am a Democrat." "I am a Republican." "I am a vegetarian." "I am a meat eater."

No, you are not any of the above. You may agree with most or all aspects of a political party, you may not include meat in your diet, but you are yourself. You exercise your choices as life keeps on unfolding: Do democrats still deserve my vote? Is this specific candidate someone I trust? You evolve in tune to a changing world.

The change-ninja is free to choose every minute. And yes, you may end up voting for the same party your entire life, but you will make the choice every time you cast your vote. The point is: you will not sign your life to anybody's ideas, philosophies or colors unless they keep making sense to you; that is, the very "you" who is in command of your ship.

What makes us act so stupidly sometimes, having to look the other way or having to justify the unjustifiable, is simply this confusion of believing that we are what we once thought was a good idea to support—when this old idea is not supportable anymore. Period, no need for conflict.

Life is a lot easier when we remove these stories from our minds. Then there is no conflict. Other feelings may arise, like disappointment, sadness or shame (when a cause is not worth our loyalty any longer), but that is a whole different subject.

The psychology of loyalty is complex, because, as I have explained, it is often triggered by the need to protect that which is familiar to us, or by the need to belong to a tribe—even if that familiarity is only minutes old. Sometimes this syndrome manifests itself so clearly that it is mind blowing. Here is one example I had while traveling with a friend:

A SHORT STORY ON INSTANT LOYALTY

While traveling downhill with a friend on a treacherous and curvy road, a bus approached us from behind and kept putting pressure on us to go faster. Eventually the desperate bus driver passed us on a dangerous curve, placing everyone on board at immense risk of an accident. Then, the bus continued to fly down the mountain road.

We caught up with the bus at a toll booth where there was a police officer. My friend rolled down his window and started telling the policeman that the bus driver should be checked for alcohol because he was driving so dangerously. To our shock, the people from inside the bus started yelling insults at us, protecting their driver.

Pledging allegiance to anything other than reality is dangerous. Power-hungry people use our weaknesses all the time by turning us into loyal soldiers to a doctrine, a flag or a territory—let alone to the idea that "our group of people is better." This danger is what we will discuss next.

BRAINWASHING

Brainwashing succeeds to some degree in all of us. Brainwashing is generally intelligently designed, well packaged and masterfully served to us. We all buy something sometimes, based on impulse, whether we are moved by a catchy ad or by a story that we decide to believe as true. If we are careful about maintaining our freedom from beliefs, and from misunderstood loyalties, our chances of not becoming victims of brainwashing are significantly better.

The potential threat of brainwashing, however, is immense and very real. A large percentage of our planet sadly suffers from this form of restraint from freedom, and they do not know it. Brainwashing serves as a lock that not only keeps people stuck from exercising their freedom, but also puts millions at the service of those skillful manipulators who are not necessarily the best leaders to follow.

Brainwashing can come from the guy in a suit or the guy with long hair and a beard with the peace sign. Brainwashing may come in the form of speech or in the form of soft music. It may come by inflicting fear in us or by offering fame and riches. Invitations to give up our freedom and join useless and dangerous loyalties prey on us all the time, in greater or lesser degrees. In the same degree, they affect our freedom.

A good exercise to avoid becoming a victim is to step back from your emotions and observe how things appeal to you by design, by color or by message. You will find it entertaining to catch yourself reacting to something designed at convincing you for the wrong reasons. Television ads? Ideologies? Movies?

But unfortunately, the intention to brainwash is not always obvious. By definition, this form of manipulation is designed to go straight to your brain and convince you about something. So, in order not to even be a potential victim of brainwashing, live a life that makes it hard to happen to you. What I am referring to is avoiding the fertile ground to becoming a prey:

- Live aware of the fact that the way you perceive something is through your cultural and upbringing filters. This means that it is smart to remember that your view on something may not be the most accurate or complete. Thus, always allow a possibility to change your view or opinion, or to learn something that can complete your views.
- Avoid falling into a cultural bubble where all the information comes from inside the same bubble. (Classic examples of this are cults and totalitarian regimes that feed their people only carefully manufactured information and prevent them from learning about other perspectives.)
- Avoid the geographic cultural bubble if you live in a large country with a large population. Even without a totalitarian regime, large countries (examples I have experienced are the U.S.A. and Brazil) tend to become bubbles by the limited amount of information about the outside. For a man in Iowa, there's a lot of information to process before he can gain interest in what is happening in Venezuela or China. Make a special effort to explore the world outside your cultural boundaries, even if it is by reading or watching videos; the best way is by living with people who are culturally different from you.
- Stay internet-smart: Cultural bubbles are not only geographic anymore. Surprisingly, the internet, which is a fabulous

window to the world, is also brilliantly utilized to generate cultural bubbles of information, by focusing you on a specific line of thinking. The result is a narrow perspective on a subject, to a point where questions are not even accepted.

- Do not be naive about social media. An era of special note has recently opened with the use of social media as a weapon of mass destruction. The recent acknowledgments from Google, Facebook and Twitter have confirmed a poisonous use of social media in the form of millions of people receiving hate-inducing messages.
- Seek opposing views to something that has impacted you positively or negatively.
- Distrust information that seems to be deliberately scaring you.
- Distrust information that generalizes human groups.
- Remember that you are not your emotions. Your emotions are part of you and you get to choose what to do with them. If you let them be your guide, you could end up in a bad situation.

THE PAYCHECK ANCHOR

Other people may not be anchored by resistance to change; rather, what keeps them in an undesirable place is simply raw necessity: necessity coupled by the absence of a strategy to break free from the cycle of salary.

Say you live from paycheck to paycheck and the instant that the flow stops, your family would starve. In his book, *The Secret Shame of Middle Class America,* Neal Gabler comments on data obtained by a survey conducted by the Federal Reserve Board which found that nearly half of Americans would have trouble if they had to pay for a four-hundred-dollar emergency. If you feel you are in this position, you have a lot of company.

But as much as there is a relief in knowing that your struggle is neither unique nor foolish, at the same time, if you are among this group, a change for the better is urgent for you. The method described in this book to transition towards a new objective, such as a new job, is designed and proven to work in an overlapping fashion. I encourage you to make a jump more like a "stretch," reaching second base without fully leaving first base. I hope this works for you.

THE RETIREMENT ANCHOR

Figuring out alternatives to secure a passive income is responsible and wise. Believing that a pension plan is a good reason to stay in a less than fulfilling job is not. The quality of your life should never be deferred for the last quarter of it.

Financial security is an undeniably desirable asset. Nothing wrong with wanting that! But one key element to living a big life precisely rides on not sticking to one activity for too many years. Of course there may be many exceptions to this (if people find fascinating diversity in their one career, for example), but this is rather fragile terrain. We must be very honest with ourselves and make sure that it is not that distant security that is holding us in a cage.

Money without having to work sounds nice. It is nice. It is wonderful, but if you read the fine print of retirement, it is not free money without working. You pay dearly for it. Generally, we pay a very expensive price for that saved money that may come sometime later in our life.

Retirement money is not bad, but it really depends on how you are paying for it. One thing you can count on is that people who have wings (because they are change-ninjas) do not stay in a job for the retirement plan... ever. They may have retirement income, but it is not the reason why they stick with one job for twenty-five years.

Change-ninjas view life differently. If you have not read *Rich Dad Poor Dad* by Robert Kiyosaki, I strongly suggest you start reading it while you continue to move toward becoming a person who is more able to change. Kiyosaki will communicate in a very practical way much of what we can say about the true cost of retirement and will provide you with a whole new approach.

It is never a good decision to cling to misery while waiting for retirement. Life is so much more than what is left of a person after eight hours is multiplied by thirty years. Just for an exercise, take a day off from work and get a sense of how many things you get done for your own projects. You will be impressed by how generous eight or nine hours really are! Couldn't you build a rocket with those hours if you only gave yourself the chance?

BEING DIFFERENT

Overcoming the fear of being different is something worth working on. This fear is a common anchor to freedom and change. If implementing an important change in your life requires you to feel somewhat different from the average, do not let that fear stop you. There was a time when being different was not necessarily being weird.

Industry and large-scale businesses in general get a significant benefit from uniformity and standardization. There's hardly any doubt about the benefits of standardization and mass production of socks, cookies, houses or sandwiches, if your goal is to maximize profit.

The problem is that standardization and uniformity as a context for human life can be poison to people's vision, creativity and ability to understand the power of change. The gods of standardization and uniformity have grown exponentially in the last half of the Twentieth Century and into this century.

Now that the internet has become a worldwide window, it is in people's hands to take advantage of this fabulous tool while not letting it further contaminate life with uniformity. Uniformity sends us an unwritten message that the limits of creativity are outlined by what is out there. Our houses, neighborhoods and cities in the United States have become dramatically alike. So has our thinking in many aspects. This environment is not good for the human spirit. The human spirit is free and wants to fly and keep creating. Even if the individual does not recognize the pressure of the context, the forces inside us are pushing outward.

The message of industry is that we are better off by wearing the same type of pants all at once. When industry decides to change our uniform, we all must follow instructions. On many occasions, important change is hindered by our fear of being different. But what is even worse is the notion that what is different is not good. That's slavery.

Time after time, humanity has to thank the visionary who was called insane, as well as the insane person who gave us a vision. The courageous ones are those who said it or did it differently. The great Greek mathematician Pythagoras, Michelangelo, Nikola Tesla and many, many more can populate a long list of visionaries.

LOSS OF INVESTMENT

When my friend David Leonard and I were in our late twenties, he was a builder, a fine woodworker and a stained glass artist. That was the image that I had of my friend. One day he announced that he was going to start attending acupuncture school and pursue a Chinese medical degree. I immediately thought of the time he had invested in those other skills and part of me felt like all that effort was now going to go to waste. That was dumb of me.

David has been a prominent doctor for over two decades now. As a person of change, David has explored several areas of medicine, he has founded a school in Hawaii, he has published several books, he teaches martial arts and he is flowing constantly within the streams of his profession and his passions.

It is never too soon to make the change you need to make, nor it is too late. It is important that you stop and be frank with yourself. Analyze the benefits of staying where you are. What is truly pulling you into inertia? Is it comfort? Is it feeling powerless to tackle the next climb? Is it the comforting idea of a retirement benefit twenty ugly years from now?

GRUDGES

Grudges can be powerful and are always stupid anchors.

When I was thirteen years old, I felt that my best friend had failed our friendship. For the next seven years I did not talk to him. We were in the same school and class. Eventually we graduated from high school and at one of the many times that we would run into each other on social occasions I approached him and offered my hand. After a few minutes I had to ask him if he remembered the reason why I had cut off our friendship so abruptly. (I did not remember!) He explained that he had refused to help me with an algebra problem in our homework. I had given up my freedom to be friends with him in order simply to stick to my position… very stupid.

I had forgotten the real reason, but I kept the story alive in my head that he did not deserve my friendship. We laughed, but it was really no laughing matter to me. I had a serious problem with grudges and forgiveness. This was a slap in the face, proof that I needed to work on it.

What did I gain by holding this grudge over seven long years? Nothing.

I came to the realization that I would never know what I had missed by not enjoying this friendship for those seven years. But I feel with overwhelming certainty that I missed hundreds of opportunities and I gained zero of anything.

My approach to grudges has since changed one-hundred-eighty degrees. I do not give a grudge the space to cause me damage. Forgiving is not always easy; sometimes the feeling that keeps the grudge alive is that the other person does not deserve my forgiveness. This may be completely true. I may not go back to the same level of relationship, but grudges have to go out the window in order for me to be free.

In reality, holding a grudge is gifting your freedom to the wrong person; precisely to the one who may not deserve it. Grudges have to go away because they are big anchors that tend to hold us not only in a confusing present, but, even worse, in a nonexistent past that we keep resituating in front of ourselves to block the door to freedom.

SMALL COMPULSIONS THAT KILL CAREERS

Our little routines and obsessions are huge career killers and assassins of change. As absurd as it sounds, many of us sacrifice a whole new career at the mercy of small foolish things that grab us like little hands one after the other. For my mom, it was having the perfect house. For my neighbor, it is his yard and for other people it is excelling at the job they hate.

Every time you stop an obsessive urge, you are gaining freedom. Many people do not realize the price they pay for believing that, for example, they cannot pick up a book while the yard does not look perfect. Just think of the many outside obsessions that may be controlling your life!

We have to learn to say no to compulsive behavior. We will talk more about this further in the chapter on Getting Things Done.

FEAR OF THE FINAL

It is hard to truly experience the essence of life's profound beauty without embracing life's material end. Without doubt, a large percentage of the human race has some degree of fear of the ultimate unknown; that is, the end of life as we know it, in our physical body. All religious and spiritual propositions speak to us of life beyond what we see and what we touch with our senses.

I will not attempt to encourage you to adopt my personal beliefs about the end of life. But I am convinced that many people cling to the past due to fear of death, thus missing exquisite opportunities to flow harmoniously with change and with time. I must invite you to visit and confront this fear of the end—if it resides somewhere inside you and acts as an anchor to healthy change. On the opposite end of the spectrum, for some people this fear is a motivator to live a life as fully as possible. In this case, you may have other reasons to face this fear and you may find that embracing death is a great way to live a truly full life.

What is important in the context of this book is that you do not avoid this important matter like a shadow in a closet; especially so if you know that fear of death is a big rock that is keeping you pinned down.

THE ERA OF CHANGE-NINJAS

It has not been until relatively recently that the conversation on leadership in the business world has awakened to the urgent need for leaders to manage creativity in such a way that it does not get killed or wasted.

Why suddenly care about creativity as a valuable asset? Because creativity is a magic wand, and it requires a mind that is agile to change to exist. It has always been there in successful enterprises, except that (just as on an individual scale) it was not considered an important and determining factor to the fate of a business.

We all have heard about many cases where rigidity was such an obviously self-poisoning attitude that certain corporations are either defunct or agonizing now. With all the money in the world, these giant businesses did not adapt to the winds of change. Remember before you forget: Kodak, Blockbuster Video, Borders Books, Sears, Pan Am Airlines, Motorola, Yahoo, Blackberry, and among many more corporations besides.

Many big companies are still around riding on the tail of the Industrial Revolution mentality. Companies built on heavy hierarchical structures of processes, scale, automation. Believers in "keep doing what we know, just at a larger scale" are nervously trying to balance their acts in this moment.

And then they will need to do it again. And again.

FAIL, FAIL, FAIL

The smartest business leaders are actively balancing the machinery of processes versus the risk-colored dragon of creativity. This is the new magic needed in management in today's innovation-driven economy. Change-ninjas in the business world are transitioning from having nothing to having superpowers, while many already huge companies are feeding on ways to use creativity and never underestimate the importance of agility to change again.

Yes, look at Amazon, Tesla, Google, Apple, and many others taking over the world absolutely based on the magic of failing. Failing? Yes, these companies have made failing a way to greatness and that is precisely the topic of conversation in the stressed meeting rooms of the corporate world.

Elan Musk does not only manage in a creative way, but he fosters creativity. He plants seeds and lets fast-moving, change-ninja creative minds create and also fail—of course! The end result, like Tesla cars, is something that we now take for granted. But who in his right mind would have started a car company in the U.S.A... When in seventy years we went from hundreds of American automakers to a handful? I guess the question is what is the "right mind?"

Failing and being wrong are never an anchor to the change-ninja. Being wrong should not have a connotation other than "one less approach to try in the future."

Many reports point to the scarcity of creative individuals in the business world. Organizations are now looking for creative individuals who are quick to adapt and are flexible. Yes, creativity is a direct result of agility to change.

I believe that many of the problems that create that scarcity of people who are agile to change are directly connected to creativity. As I describe in the Enjoy Your Wings chapter in this book, creativity is one of the things that people who are change-ninjas benefit from. Most of us underestimate the power of remaining flexible and being quick to adapt to change, let alone practice and actively become an individual prone to change.

YOUR RELATIONSHIP WITH FAILURE

When we become adults, a negative relationship with failure is directly conducive to finding a safe little space, making a nest, and avoiding venturing out into the world so that we never ever have to be exposed again to the shame of being wrong. Change is the last thing you want to attempt when you are afraid of making a mistake.

This attitude makes a person cling to the first acceptable thing that feels safe—a career, a job, a way of life—often sentencing the person to a tiny life. But "failure" is truly only a label of choice. What counts is our reaction to the failed attempt. "An expert is a person who has made all the mistakes that can be made in a very narrow field," said Biels Bohr, a Nobel laureate in physics. Learn to fail. Also learn to start preparing immediately for your next attempt.

Walter Elias Disney, a son of Spanish immigrants, was fired from at least one newspaper for lacking creative ideas, then formed a company, Laugh-O-Gram Films. He had to close Laugh-O-Gram down. The Walt Disney we hear about is the "genius" who built an empire. This was a man who would not get stuck due to fear of failure or to failure itself, just like the following examples picked among thousands of possible examples:

- Arianna Huffington was rejected by more than thirty publishers before launching *The Huffington Post*.
- Lawrence Ellison dropped out of college and worked as a programmer for eight years. He cofounded Oracle and struggled for eight years before getting positive results.

- Before finally having one good electric bulb for the world, Thomas Alba Edison attempted over nine-thousand other ways to make it work.

- Henry Ford flunked twice with automotive companies before succeeding with what eventually placed him in a privileged spot in world history.

- Colonel Sanders founded Kentucky Fried Chicken in his late fifties. His recipe was reportedly rejected more than one-thousand times before the doors of success opened up for him.

- A college professor told Fred Smith, Fed-Ex's founder, that his business concept was interesting but not feasible.

- Bill Gates first failed with Traf-O-Data, and, after a long and painful chain of uncertainty and trial and error, he created his first Microsoft product.

- Steve Jobs's contributions to the world are the result of a person who found nourishment in failure. He learned how to successfully go from point A to point B. Apple became a massive empire, and then at thirty he was fired from his company. Subsequently, he founded NeXT, and the he came back to Apple with all the force built by his trials and errors. Once back at Apple, Steve proved his capacity for greatness by reinventing the company's image and taking the Apple brand to new heights.

THE BRAKES ON CHANGE AND CREATIVITY

Many good schools and many good teachers foster creativity. But, the natural change-ninjas in our world's too-many poor school systems have to painfully endure the fourteen years from pre-K to graduation. They either drop out or survive using their personal creativity. Once they are free, they thrive.

I am not an expert on education, but I am absolutely certain that many of the good intentions poured into our education system are not conducive to encouraging and keeping fundamental freedoms alive in children. Instead, schools do the exact opposite, often completely discouraging children from making mistakes in their learning process. (What a contradiction! How else can you learn?)

Education needs to be reformed and, in the meantime, parents have a duty to keep their children protected from the destructive aspects of education as we know it.

In terms of a direction toward reform of the education system, I strongly agree with Sir Ken Robinson's analysis and proposals. Education expert and author, Robinson brilliantly observes how the educational system penalizes failure, and children simply grow up frightened of being wrong.

READY TO CHANGE BUT CLUELESS ABOUT HOW

Many people are ready to move out of their comfort zone in order to change a life situation (i.e., to start their own business or to change careers or jobs), but they do not have clarity about direction and/or they do not have a map or a method to get there effectively.

Having a map helps us a great deal. Just like having a sense of direction in the physical world, when we have directions we perform better. We find destinations faster and less painfully in a city where we do not know our way around. This book will help you build your own map to make change easier.

It is very common for most people not to have a method or a map to make major changes in their lives, because most of us get to a specific point in adulthood as a result of circumstances where we have not exercised much control. In other words, how most people got to where they are now is not the result of a fully conscious decision and a chartered journey. Life often leads us through a series of moments that little by little define the course of our journey and bring us to where we are—and we do not always feel in harmony with that place where we are parked.

Millions live in that place where their lives have brought them. Some are happy and fulfilled while some are unhappy and unsatisfied.

Making changes leading to a more harmonious place in your world will make you happier, and it will also make you a more productive and successful person. And, all that comes hand in hand with big side benefits: mental, emotional and physical health.

This can even get more exciting: If you learn to manage change in a constant fashion in your life, you will experience doors opening to allow you to accomplish things that you perhaps thought were not within your reach. You will have the most critical tool to be successful at what you want to be. You will live a more meaningful life every day.

> "Start by doing what is necessary; then do what is possible and soon you will be doing the impossible."
> Francis of Assisi

COMMANDING CHANGE IN YOUR LIFE

So, by now you know that this book's mission is not only to help you make that one important change that you have been trying to make for months or years, but also to open the eyes of your soul and mind to a new way of living your life: always free, always evolving in different dimensions, and seizing the moment in ways that your entire being vibrates with life.

COMMANDER OF INTENTION

No person is in complete control of his or her fate, but there are plenty of good opportunities provided by fate itself for us to set our own direction.

We need a general direction in order to navigate, and then we need a map and then we need a strategy to get there, amid a voracious jungle of distractions. And if arguably no human being is in control of his destiny, you certainly own the power of intention. Just like you own the freedom to daydream, most importantly, you own the freedom to state your intention to go from point A to point B. And that is no insignificant power in your hands. Intention is powerful; wishful thinking is not.

Magic happens when you define your objective and turn it into an intention. Of course there is no flying carpet that will pick you up and take you to your objective, but there are things that get set in motion around you, after you manifest intention.

The power of intention is like shooting an arrow that shows the direction to a specific target. Then, you can follow the path created by that arrow and eventually arrive at goal. The arrow causes an invisible path to exist. In some dimension, this path makes a difference. Once your intention has been manifested, very often, things start to occur in your life that seem to reinforce or facilitate the actual accomplishment of the objective.

Perhaps to be more scientific, I may explain the power of intention as having crossed that fine line between "wishing" and "knowing" that you can actually do it. The knowing holds the power.

Finally, the other side of the coin of this power is not to be ignored: Before you manifest your intention, do all the necessary homework in regards to the foundation to your decision. This is a subtle theme that can be difficult to grasp, so allow me to go a little deeper.

INTENTION VERSUS WISHING

Intention is not a wish. There's nothing wrong with wishing, but intention is a different animal. Like a bee to a leopard, like an elephant to a mouse. Different.

Intention is a state of preparing to take physical action in this universe while setting a subtle internal mechanism in motion. Intention has certainty built in.

Intention happens when you plan on going to the store and you know you have a few more things to finish at home but you are going to the store. If your friend calls you on the phone and you say, "I am going to the store in a few more minutes," that is intention. Intention is a steady purpose that only changes due to something major and out of your control: a flash flood in your street; a traffic accident on your way to the store. The derailing has to be unavoidable, otherwise you are going to the store. That's intention.

On the other hand, considering going to the store is one-hundred percent different. Something vital has not clicked yet. If you are considering going to the store, many other tasks may also have the same level of priority, and it may turn out that you simply do not go to the store at all and life moves on without major consequences.

Wishing for something is just the desire to have something. Of course, in order to move in any direction or in order to take action towards attaining something, it is necessary to have that feeling called wishing. But we can wish all day long sitting in front of a magazine, a computer screen, or pondering in our head, and the chances of a new life arriving as a package falling through our roof and onto our laps are very, very remote—to put it lightly.

If you pay attention to the people around you, you will hear a lot of "I should…" and then those who say "I will …". That is the difference.

And, if you are a person who lives around animals, I am going to give you an extra tool to help you understand intention. Some animals read our intention very clearly. (I have only tried with dogs and horses.) Notice how your animal reacts to an idea about going to the park versus a decision to go to the park. Both processes are inside you, with no words said. I started experimenting and observing this thanks to my good friends Jean Jacques and Isabelle who practice psychotherapy with the aid of horses in Boulder, Colorado.

PRACTICING TO BECOME A CHANGE-NINJA

To be a "natural" at something is often understood as to be born with a specific quality. Let's disarm this myth immediately. If we carefully look at what science knows as of this moment, we should conclude that we come into this world with a pretty much empty brain.

Throughout life, our brain learns, changes and adapts wonderfully to new learning when we push it.

If by now you agree that the best way to live is by being a creature of change, you may want to start with exercises that may seem very insignificant at first sight. However, they are designed to break habits and breaking habits is a fundamental step to living the free and exciting life you most want for yourself.

HABIT BREAKING, HABIT CREATING

Habits tend to creep in and start building rigidity around our daily life just like weeds creep into a garden. Yet, ironically, we need to create new habits sometimes in order to accomplish major changes. This seems contradictory, but the moment you have mastered breaking old habits and creating new ones at will, you will have become quite a powerful person. Also, "good" habits can help to create perseverance—another useful tool to accomplishing big goals.

Dr. Joe Z. Tsien, Co-Director of the Brain and Behavior Discovery Institute at Georgia Health Sciences University, published a pertinent study in 2011. Dr. Tsien's main point is that dopamine neurons regulate circuits throughout the brain. He believes that this discovery opens the door to speeding up the process of forming good habits and, possibly, selectively removing bad ones such as drug addiction or smoking, since the same circuits are seemingly involved in both. The experiment is much more complex and it involves blocking certain areas of the brain from receiving the dopamine that flows when we are doing something pleasant in "automatic mode." But for our purposes, the theory is that once we repeat something enough times for it to become a habit, it will bring us pleasure... Very useful for things like exercising.

The habits I will suggest that you break next should be innocuous, but they serve the purpose of training you to be flexible while training your brain as well. You do not have to change the exact habits that follow as examples. Feel free to examine your own day and just for the fun of it, start changing one or two of those small, yet constant things you do absolutely unconsciously. The only requirement is that you work to change things you perform in auto-mode.

Here are examples of things you can change that that are a good start for training your mind to be more flexible:

DAILY PRACTICE

We can become more agile to change by getting used to constant change. Walk through your day watching how easily you fall into routines. Some may be necessary to make your life more efficient, but many are built automatically and maintained unconsciously. These are the ones where we can have fun with, first discovering them and then changing them as a form of exercise. Below are some examples; you can uncover many more.

Change your route to work or school and back, every day. If you cannot alter the route, add a little loop to it. (I.e., Stop at a bookstore or another store. Walk around a park before hopping on the train or bus.) You can also change your desk, your coffee mug, or the decor in your office.

Interrupt a typical daily routine and carefully analyze a plant, animal or insect in detail. This can be a tree in your yard, your dog or your cat. The requirement is that you observe something beyond the point you used to notice it before.

Other ideas for changes in daily routines: Brush your teeth with the other hand. Comb your hair with the other hand. Hold your phone with the other hand. Use your computer mouse with the other hand. Wash dishes with the other hand. Hold your glass or your cup with the other hand, and drink from it. Try different places for coffee or lunch. Try a different food that has never even caught your interest before. If you watch a lot of YouTube, set a timer, when it rings, stop watching and change to a physical activity; for example, clean your house or walk or bike.

WEEK-BY-WEEK PRACTICE

Find a weekly routine that you have and change it. The more discomfort that this idea of change seems to create for you, the more you will benefit from the exercise. And know that eventually you will also get pleasure from these changes just as you get pleasure from established activities, with one huge caveat: Your life will expand beyond just the new activity.

It is very important that you do not interpret this exercise as simply an introduction to a new sport or hobby. This is about liberating deeper areas inside you by breaking a routine. These exercises will wake up areas completely dormant in many people, and extremely important to expanding life to a more fulfilling level.

Skip your yard work routine and hire someone to do it. Or, find something that you do approximately every two weeks and skip it. Then create a completely new pattern around the activity. Buy flowers for someone you appreciate. Out of the blue, for no reason, surprise the person.

Engage in conversation with a stranger. Even if this means extending your conversation with the gas station attendant. Do this by showing interest in his work or something that you believe may be important to this stranger.

Ride the bus to work instead of driving. Keep this change for a while.

If you go with your spouse to the movies on Mondays, skip one Monday and do something radically different that you have never done before. (I.e., go watch a live sporting event, enjoy live music, go for a drink, or walk through a park you did not know existed.)

SIX-MONTH PRACTICE

Introduce a new color into your wardrobe, preferably the most divergent from your typical colors. Change your dress style or hair style. Travel to places near where you live. Listen to a different kind of music than usual. Pick a different read. Listen to a different radio station for part of the day... dangerous! Make a plan to travel abroad for a week or a long weekend.

YEARLY PRACTICE

Take up a new sport or recreational activity. If you golf, buy a drone. If you have never gone to a gym, join one. Start running or hiking. Pick a radically new activity that you only watch online, and actually do it. Start a new hobby. If you do not have an artistic hobby, buy some basic acrylic colors and paint a piece of wood. (Start with something small first.)

If you are always feeling frustrated with computers, learn one basic software application in depth. Even if it is Word, learn all aspects of it. Travel to a foreign country, and stay with the local people. Learn to play one instrument. Switch to a different car.

> "The world is a book and those who do not travel read only a page." St. Augustine

FIVE-YEAR PRACTICE

Change jobs. Learn a new language. Move to a different place. Go back to school. Change careers. (Be aware that most of these will require some planning and moving things in your life, but decide to do it and then make a plan and go for it.)

WHAT IS THE PURPOSE?

The purpose of these examples and ideas of exercises is to:

93

A) Gain awareness of how many things you do on autopilot.

B) Notice how many activities keep you stuck in your life, when you could have wings and travel freely.

C) Force conscious change of these repetitive patterns and teach your subconscious to exercise change at all levels, as frequently as possible, in small and large things.

D) Eventually reap the many benefits of becoming a natural at change. As a natural at change, all these exercises should become a way of life and the results should begin to show in your life in unexpected manners; for instance, by being able to enjoy certain things you did not enjoy before, or by making changes in markedly more swiftly, to your own surprise.

A HEALTHY BRAIN

It is not my aim to discuss neuroscience in depth here. I simply wish to make a recommendation that will not hurt anyone. If you want to become a creative person and a change-ninja, of course you want to keep your brain in tip-top shape. It also helps to know what science says about your brain, and I strongly recommend to look for good, reliable current information about the capabilities of your brain. (Not your neighbor's or Einstein's brain. Your brain.)

If you are skeptical about your brain's ability to change at a certain age, it will encourage you to know that people are actually built for change. As neuroscientist Michael Merzenich, whom we discussed previously, clearly explains in his 2004 Ted Talk, your brain is constructed for change. It is all about change. Change confers on us the ability to do things tomorrow that we cannot do today, to do things today that we couldn't do yesterday.

Merzenich looks at one of the secrets of the brain's incredible power: its ability to actively re-wire itself. He is currently researching ways to harness the brain's plasticity to enhance our skills and recover lost function. After his extensive research, Merzenich's position is that science is telling us we are in charge, and that it is time to accept that our happiness, our well-being, and our abilities are capable of continuous modification and improvement. Our ability to change is our responsibility.

While it is beyond the scope of this book to dig deeper into Merzenich's work, I highly recommend that you look on your own into his brain-training program.

BROAD SPECTRUM EXERCISES FOR THE LEFT HEMISPHERE

Play chess, do crossword puzzles, other kind of puzzles, and Sudoku. Write a short article about your favorite subject. Learn a new language. Read books in depth (without skimming pages). Organize your day with a logical list of chores written in order, for instance, by geographical proximity. Learn a new skill.

BROAD SPECTRUM EXERCISES FOR THE RIGHT HEMISPHERE

Play a musical instrument. Paint; sketch; dance; doodle. Practice memory games such as reading half a page of a story and repeating it faithfully. Or memorize a room, close your eyes, and describe it. Build things with your hands. Try carving or Origami. Ride a bike, visualizing a strategy to go over a piece of terrain and following through on a mental plan with action.

SURVIVING THE JUNGLE OF DISTRACTIONS

If we want to accomplish something over a period of time, such as a career change or a major change in our lives, we cannot take today's universe of distraction lightly.

All over the planet, increasingly more buildings are filled with computers, all holding more and more data. The world has changed beyond our imagination. We have not had enough generations growing up under so much power of distraction yet to know the kind of impact it may make to have the world in our pocket.

German E. Velasco

We are raising children who have: television, movie theaters, libraries, intercontinental phone lines, voices of thousands of people wanting to share silly information, voices of people wanting to share brilliant information—from the other end of the world, from next door—dumb games, fabulous games, horrible information, fabulous information, small and big information about friends renewed by the minute, regular news, sports, and much more. All in their pockets.

Life is a jungle of distractions. From the moment we wake up to the moment we go back to bed we are challenged by far more elements than walking in a real jungle in South America.

About fifty hours of content are uploaded to YouTube every second. A person could live a lifetime watching YouTube videos without ever repeating a single one.

But none of us will harness the power of this fabulous tool—social media—simply by aimlessly browsing. The potential of the internet is fantastic as a tool, and so is its potential as a destructive weapon. But at this moment what concerns us is that in order to get things done in your life, you have to be very careful not to fall into the distractive vortex of the internet.

Scarier than walking through life overwhelmed with distractions is being deprived of moments of plain, empty boredom. Modern life has cancelled that door to healthy emptiness and the consequent invitation to explore deeper areas of the self.

Clicking the icon on the screen has cancelled the opportunity to feel what we feel—especially when it is uncomfortable. That's where our inner self is desperately asking for changes, or where we find those pains that we need to heal in order to advance.

The next chapter deals head-on with the jungle of distractions. It provides specific tools to save yourself from one of your dreams' greatest enemies.

11
THE MAGIC TOWER

When I think of an old castle's tower, there are two important qualities that I find in this kind of building. One is its isolation. The other attribute is its strategic positioning for extended visibility. Ships had towers, castles had towers, and there are observation towers of all kinds. Thus, my choice for the name of the tool I am about to describe to you.

This tool, the magic tower, can help you accomplish deep changes inside you, or help you meet very specific goals like switching jobs, writing a book or managing your time and energy much more effectively. From your tower, you will be able to see if where you are headed is where you really want to go. This will allow you to make adjustments in moving toward your goals. Also, you will lay out a path toward those goals in specific and down-to-earth steps.

Sometimes you will find truly fascinating new insights about yourself and your projects from the comfort of your tower. Then you will make any necessary adjustments for when you go back to your normal busy and distracted life. Sometimes you may find discomforting sensations while in the tower, that you were not aware of before. It will be extremely important to stop and pay attention to those sensations, because while they may not be pleasant, they are always a gift. Your body manifests everything, and pinpointing and confronting any negative inner feelings can help you to become healthier.

Oh! And why "magic"? Because this tool produces outstanding results with relatively little effort—my very personal understanding of the meaning of magic.

So, what exactly is your magic tower? It is a timed activity and an exercise of your imagination. Your magic tower consists, quite simply, of (1) two hours per week in a space without distractions, and (2) a pencil and some graph paper. These two hours will allow you to see far inside your own life's perspective: past, present and possible future. In this space and time, you will perform all the planning for achieving your goals—from broad idea, to narrow concept and action; from the big picture to the individual task. You will find, once you have your goals clearly broken down into a series of day-to-day tasks, that you can trust that you are on the right path and avoid a great dose of unnecessary stress. No matter how busy and confusing your day gets, you will know that the guidance that comes from your magic tower is reliable. You will be able to make steady and automatic progress toward your goals without having to revisit them.

CREATING YOUR TOWER: THE PHYSICAL SPACE

To undertake this exercise, you will need a place where you can write and think and be free of distractions. Your magic tower does not always have to be the same physical place (you can access your tower from any place on earth,) but at first, until you are better able to exercise your powers of concentration, the physical location of your magic tower should be quite isolated.

If you like to listen to music while you work, please make an exception and do not listen to music in the magic tower. If you find this experience to be too isolating, try listening to classical or instrumental music with no lyrics and with the volume set low. With time, you may find that your powers of introspection have become so strong that you can even visit your magic tower from a coffee shop... but this will not be the case initially.

LENGTH OF TIME IN YOUR TOWER

You should plan to spend two hours per week in your magic tower. You can devote this time all at once, or, you may want to experience your magic tower two times per week for an hour each time. Whenever you decide it is the moment to work in your magic tower, set an alarm so that you are free of the distraction of continuously checking how much time has passed.

The exercises that follow will all take place in your magic tower, but they will probably not take place in one session. Use your own judgement to determine how long each session in your magic tower should last, and how much you can comfortably accomplish in each session.

MINDFULNESS IN THE TOWER

The Google Dictionary definition of mindfulness is, "a mental state achieved by focusing one's awareness on the present moment, while calmly acknowledging and accepting one's feelings, thoughts, and bodily sensations, used as a therapeutic technique." Your first objective in your magic tower is to achieve a state of mindfulness. This state will allow you to be deeply introspective and more aware of your inner desires, anchors, fears and goals.

Start by relaxing your feet, then your legs, and eventually your entire body part by part. Allow your muscles to relax, and focus on each part of your body with your mind. Spend some moments concentrating on your breathing, and allow your breathing to slow. In your mind, envelope your body with light.

Next, picture your magic tower in your mind, and create it in any fashion you like. Your tower should look pleasant to you. Personally, I like to visualize a white tower like a lighthouse. I've become so familiar with my tower by now that I can see it quite clearly even as I write this.

Then, see and feel that you are on the top floor of that tower in a very personal space. You are deeply comfortable, cocooned in light, and you have total peace of mind. You are safe and your environment is a positive one in every respect.

In this space, create a big screen or window. Through this window or on this screen, observe yourself living your normal life.

From this moment on, once you reach this point in your magic tower exercise, you will interact with the everyday you whom you are observing. You will take time to feel what the everyday you is feeling. You will be able to perceive what this everyday you thinks and needs and wants. From your vantage point in the magic tower, you will be able to find solutions to your everyday you's problems and open doors to your everyday you's dreams and desires.

DEFINE YOUR GOAL

Your magic tower is, fundamentally, a place where you realize change. Once you are in a mindful state, and once you can see your everyday you, allow your mind to contemplate the ways in which that everyday you yearns for change. As soon as you identify the areas that need change, it will naturally follow that you are able to set a goal.

A goal must be defined with enough clarity that you know the direction in which you are going. If you find yourself saying, "I would like to go into something like engineering," or "I need a different job," or "I hate this town and I wish I could live in a nicer place," or "I need to make more money," these statements are not conducive to effective change, as they are mostly wishes. They need sharpening: Your subconscious knows when you do not have a specific destination and, without this specific definition, you will not experience the drive you need.

The goals that will set you in motion should be more like these: "I am going back to school and will get a degree in civil engineering."

"I will work on my relationship with my spouse until I feel happy and comfortable again." "I will write a book on the secret life of elephants, and I will get it done in one year."

Once you have identified your goal, write it down on your piece of paper. The very act of defining and writing down your goal should give the "reward system" of your brain—a neurobiological system that regulates pleasure—a wonderful jolt of the neurotransmitter, dopamine. This dopamine will make you feel pleasure. In that moment, you will know you can achieve your goal.

WORKING WITH FEARS

After you have defined your goal, it is normal at some point to start experiencing some anxiety. The anxiety may come from thoughts that begin jumping at you: thoughts that you are not ready, thoughts that you may not be in control of a new situation, thoughts that you may lack competence to do a new thing.

Yes, all of these thoughts or similar forms of sabotage may come to you, but do not panic. From the state of mindfulness in your magic tower, let these ideas pass through you. Recognize them as empty fables, and realize the future does not exist yet. The negative thoughts cannot be taken seriously. They are at best a form of fear and, from your magic tower, you will arrive at an understanding of how to accomplish your goals even if you do feel fear. Most of the fears will dissolve in time as you start to walk down the new path you have chosen for yourself.

Often, a helpful exercise is to use your pen and paper to list your fears. Next, working from your list, contemplate each fear individually. In your mind, have a conversation with each fear. For example, if you have decided that you will go back to school to earn a civil engineering degree, you may feel afraid that you will waste a large amount of money: Tell the fear that this money is being invested, not wasted. Tell the fear that you were always good at math and science in school, so there is no reason to expect that you will not graduate from your engineering program. Tell your fear that once you are an engineer you will be in a significantly higher earning bracket.

When confronted, most fears lose power. In part, they lose power because you force them to have boundaries and to take shape. An un-faced fear is a shapeless notion lurking somewhere in the depths of your mind, annoying you at its own pace and will. Once you have defined your fear and sat down to analyze it, most likely you will realize that your imaginings of a worst-case scenario are very unlikely to become a reality.

YOUR GOAL IS URGENT

"My day gets consumed by so many household chores that I don't have time to read my book," my mother, who is a house-cleaning perfectionist, used to complain.

Actually, we all can find time for that extra effort that will get us out of our stagnation. It is simply a matter of setting priorities. When my mother had to go to an appointment or had to take one of us children to the doctor, she dropped everything. The cleanliness of the wood floors or the shine of the refrigerator took a distant second place to the urgency of getting the crying kid to the doctor.

That is how urgent your goal is... Your goal is as urgent as a visit to the doctor. Your kitchen floor, your yard or your current boss probably do not care at all about how you are going to feel thirty years from now. They do not have to. So, it is your responsibility and only yours to prioritize your goal. Take action, and make your project a truly urgent priority.

PAPER, PEN AND YOUR GOAL

Some years ago, Forbes conducted extensive research into the top ten job skills employers look for. The number-one skill was critical thinking, and the number-two skill was complex problem solving.

What is important for our purposes is that both of these skills are connected to the use of our hand on paper while thinking. Neuroscientists have found that writing with your hand leads to coordination between the right and left sides of the brain and to the boosting of cognitive skills. Using pen and paper in the environment of the magic tower amplifies your creativity and strengthens your ability to connect where you are now to where you want to be in the future.

THINKING SHEET

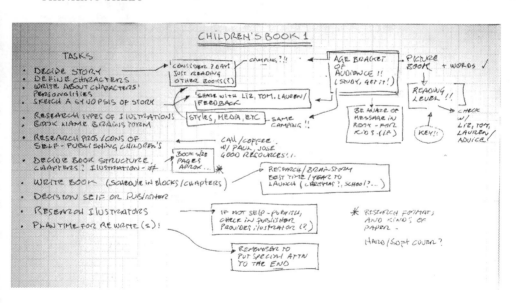

Using a fresh piece of paper, write down your goal as a heading at the top of the sheet. I like to use an 11- by 17-inch sheet of gridded paper. The grid can help to maintain some order amid what may look like chaos to others, but what will quickly become a diagram of your goals for you and only you. In your state of relaxation and mindfulness, try to write down everything you need to do to reach your goal. Do not worry about being organized or putting tasks in chronological order; order is not important at this point. At this point, you want to be thinking multidimensionally and not rejecting any ideas that may have to do in any way with translating your goal into a project. You may create a small extra frame for notes (see drawing). It truly is a thinking page. Remember, even if being clean and organized is your obsession, esthetics are not the objective of a thinking page. Freedom to accompany your powerful thinking is the objective of this page. You will organize your thoughts with precision in the next step. For now, just brainstorm.

SETTING DEADLINES

Now that you have brainstormed what you need to do to reach your goal, it is time to set deadlines based on your diagram. Setting deadlines will allow you to proceed steadily toward your goal— without much thought or additional planning once you are in the hustle and bustle of the world outside your magic tower.

"Deadline map"

MONTH 1	MONTH 5	MONTH 4	MONTH 3	MONTH 2
COMPLETE 30% WRITING ↓	MANUSCRIPT TO PUBLISHER (OR SELF-PUBLISHING PLATFORM) ↑	All WRITING DONE	COMPLETE 90% OF WRITING	COMPLETE 60% OF WRITING
DECIDE PUBLISHING METHOD ↑	FINAL REVISION ↑	All ILLUSTRATIONS OK'D (BY ME) ↑	(LEAVE AMPLE TIME FOR FINAL 10% !!)	
BOOK LENGTH DECIDED	PRE-FINAL REVISION WITH/BY EDITOR ↑	FINISH 100% OF CHAPTERS	All DECISIONS ABOUT PUBLISHING, WHO, WHERE, ETC.	
DEFINE STORY	FINAL REVISION BY CLOSE FRIENDS/ LIZ, TOM, LAUREN	CONFIRM DEADLINE WITH PUBLISHER/ HAVE PLATFORM READY	FINALIZED (CONTRACTS, PAYMENTS, ARRANGEMENTS ALL INCLUDED)	
DEFINE MAIN CHARACTERS		FINAL REVISION OF ILLUSTRATIONS WITH ILLUSTRATOR/ DESIGNER	LAST REVIEWS/ THINKING OF FORMATS	
ALL OTHER-BOOKS IDEAS/STUDY, AUDIENCE AGE 100% DEFINED		All BOOK-FORMAT DECISIONS MADE ↑	ILLUSTRATIONS COMPLETED 90%	
		FINALIZE LAST 10% OF BOOK		

Use a fresh piece of 11- by 17-inch paper, oriented horizontally, and refer to your diagram. Write the final major step needed to meet your goal in the left two inches of your sheet. For example, if you want to write and self-publish an illustrated young adult's book, your final step may be: *Market book with blogs, FaceBook and press release.*

Now, fold two inches of the sheet to the left, so that your first goal is behind the fold and you are again writing on fresh paper. In the left two inches of the sheet, write down your next-to-last step. This might be: *Upload final e-manuscript and hardcopy version to self-publishing platform.*

Continue in this manner until you have written down all the major steps to your goal. Following this example, they might be:

> *Final revision of manuscript with copy-editor. Final revision of illustrations with graphic designer.*
>
> *Finish writing last 30% of book. Provide final 30% of text to illustrator.*
>
> *Finish writing 70% of book. Keep illustrator up to date.*
>
> *Finish the first 30% of the book. Give text to illustrator.*
>
> *Decide approximate book length. Choose illustrator. Sign contract.*
>
> *Research illustrators. Contact three or four.*
>
> *Define story and title. Sketch the first ideas of story. Define characters and write a little about each character.*

This has become your deadline map. You can consider each fold in the paper a month or, if you need more time, consider each fold forty-five days or even two months. Following our example, let's call each fold two months. So, we have nine deadlines adding up to eighteen months. In eighteen months you hope to have people actually buying your book.

DAILY AGENDA

Next, you need to work on your daily agenda. For your daily agenda, you will break down your deadline map into discreet, actionable items. The number of chores that you put into your daily agenda must be realistic and should be written in direct coordination with your deadline map. This pairing will allow you to be informed and realistic about meeting your ultimate goal. It may, for example, clearly show that you need to work over a weekend or to take a day off from work.

I like using Google Calendar, but you may prefer your paper calendar or a different scheduling tool. For our sample self-publishing project, a few days of the agenda might look something like this:

July 14

Noon: *Buy large notebook and good pens for book sketches, ideas.*

12:30: *Visit bookstores, peruse young adult books. Create document in computer.*

July 15

7:00 to 9:00 a.m.: *Sketch story ideas.*

July 16

7:00 to 9:00 a.m.: *Sketch story ideas.*

July 18

7:00 to 9:00 a.m.: *Brainstorm book name.*

July 19

7:00 to 9:00 a.m.: *Brainstorm book name, make decision.*

July 20

> 7:00 to 9:00 a.m.: *Start developing characters' personalities.*

> Noon: *Check illustrators' websites, take notes.*

July 22

> 8:00 to 1:00 p.m.: *Draft first chapter of book.*

CLIMBING THE MOUNTAIN

Writing out the major steps to completing your goal, along with the daily agenda items for completing those steps, helps you in two ways. First, by establishing a series of actionable items, a goal that may have seemed as unlikely as climbing Mount Everest now transforms into something very possible. Second, each time you complete an agenda item, the reward system of the brain will give you another satisfying boost of dopamine. What was a daunting and unformed idea is now a clear and constantly enjoyable journey.

OUTSIDE THE TOWER: MAKE YOURSELF ACCOUNTABLE

Once you have completed your work in the magic tower, you may want to use a little trick that works for many people: Announce your goal to friends you trust, your spouse or your community. This will give you the extra kick on those Sunday mornings when you feel like you deserve to sleep in two hours because you have worked so hard all week (at the job you hate). This expectation from others around you will be the extra reminder that nobody cares how tired you feel on Sunday morning. You have things to do, very clearly marked in your agenda. Get up.

THE MILLION-DOLLAR CALL

You've learned now how to create and use your own magic tower and how to plan out the steps that will lead to your goal. These steps will run the gamut from making phone calls to writing e-mails, and they are all self-imposed tasks from your own agenda.

One of these phone calls or e-mails may very well lead to something big. One of these calls or e-mails could be the one that catapults your project to the stars. Why not? You might hit on the million-dollar call. Million-dollar calls are those causality encounters in life that, when you look back on them, you think, *Wow, if the bus in front of me had not been so slow, I wouldn't have arrived at the coffee shop later than usual. I would have never met the person who became my wife, and I would not have my wonderful children today.*

Hence, my advice to you is: Don't miss tasks once they are carefully inserted into your daily agenda with mindfulness and imagination. Don't skip a single one, because every one represents a unique chance to carry you to stunning success.

> "The true sign of intelligence is not knowledge but imagination." Albert Einstein

HAPPY WITHOUT PERMISSION

Finally, I want to close the journey of this book with an important reminder: When seeking change, make sure that you move forward by looking inside yourself. If you look inside yourself, you will make the changes that are right for you and for your happiness. At the same time, you will avoid those changes that are guided by an illusion that happiness comes from outside.

Deep inside you is the true you: The one who is not the coat you are wearing, or the profession your are known by, or any other role you are playing at a given moment in society. The true you is the one who does not mistakenly define happiness as a function of something outside of yourself. The true you does not need anybody's permission to be happy.

Too often in my coaching, I deal with clients whose source of unhappiness is an emotional dependency on a partner. If they do not feel loved, they crumble to pieces. Falling apart from unrequited love is less a sign of weakness and more a question of misplaced expectations. It is not your partner's job to make you happy. Once you truly see this, you will discover your right to be happy.

Another common mistake is to equate money with happiness. All the money in the world will not make your true self happy. On the contrary, it may distract you from what you really need to feel satisfied inside.

Then there are the other mistakes we have discussed in this book: the other anchors that hold us back such as past traumas, fears, and routines that have outlived their worth. By now, you have learned simple steps that you can take—steps as simple as combing your hair with the other hand—that can lead you, one after the other, to the place where you are a true ninja of change.

By now I hope you understand that change is inextricably tied to happiness. Life changes around us all the time, whether we want it to or not. If you learn how to sail on the winds of change, you will encounter great joy. The joy can start right now. Yes, at this very moment.

THE END